I0462807

History of World Banking
An Asian Perspective

MAINE-PATRIOT.com
3 Linnell Circle
Brunswick, Maine 04011

maine-patriot.com

Where did King Solomon's Treasure Go?

History of World Banking

History of World Banking
An Asian Perspective

Contents

Appendix

Republic for the united States of America

History of World Banking

Introduction

The following information was gathered over the years, by talking to people with personal and unique experience in the *secret service* of World Finance . . .

. . . older people who have lived secret lives in hiding for the last 50 years while controlling the Gold certificates and Key accounts upon which the modern system of world Banking has been built.

This is their version of History. A simplified story of evil versus good, but it's never quite that simple, for the battles and the players are more complex. Most of this story is playing out in the gray area between right and wrong.

Regardless. We think it important for everyone to know where the World is heading financially today, for important choices regarding the future must be made.

History of World Banking

1
History of World Banking

It started with King Solomon, in Jerusalem, around 930 B.C. Solomon was a very successful King who amassed huge wealth . . . especially gold.

He had 600 wives & concubines and thousands of children.

Knowing that his country would fall apart after his death, he selected one of his most trusted wives, Queen Shaba, or Balquish, to protect his assets, bloodline, and traditions thereafter.

Sometime later, she leaves Jerusalem taking everything back to where she came from: Java.

There she establishes the Courts of what later become known as Solo Jawa . . . there safeguarding the gold assets, King Solomon's bloodline, and the religious traditions of his court.

The Gold pile grows

Huge flows of gold from China into Indonesia take place during the 1300's. China almost goes broke buying spices; and wood.

In the 1400–1600's, most of the gold from Europe — taken from South America — ends up in Indonesia as payment for spices; the most sought after goods at that time.

The Royal Solo family ties expand to include the Chinese Royals.

1000 A.D.

A few "Knights" spend 9 years in Jerusalem digging out the ruins of King Solomon's Temple.

They discover something that makes them very powerful once they return to Europe.

They get special privileges from the Pope. This leads to The Knights Templar Order being established with direct access to the Pope.

• The Knights Templar quickly become Europe's protector of wealth, and of the pilgrims traveling to Jerusalem.

• This leads to the establishment of the first Banking system, working throughout the European world.

• People of means deposit their wealth with the Knights Templar and then draw from it when they are in the "Holy Land" or on the road back home.

1064 A.D.

• The Knights Templar first establish a connection with the old King Solomon bloodline in Solo Jawa.

- They discover something that makes them very powerful once back in Europe.

Friday the 13th, October, 1307.

The Templars are now rich, powerful, and independent from European church and state organizations.

The French King, together with the Pope, conspires to confiscate their assets and destroy their power. All over Europe, on Friday the 13th, October, 1307, the Templars are hunted down, jailed, and many are killed, and their land holdings and assets are confiscated.

The Templars hide and flee in three main directions.

One group flees into the mountains of central Europe to what eventually becomes Switzerland.

One group flees north and establishes a safe haven in northern Scotland, and in Scandinavia, while the third group flees west to Portugal, from where they eventually migrate to America.

1400-1500 A.D.

The Templar group in Scotland leave and travel to Indonesia where they set up a base at Madura and unite with the Solomon bloodline in Solo Jawa.

1600-1700 A.D.

The Templars in Solo Jawa, together with their brothers in the Alps, start issuing paper certificates backed by gold . . . a piece of paper that represents a certain amount of gold, which can be easily moved about and lent out.

Interest was 2-3% per year payable in gold.

1700-1800 A.D.

One German banker, backing a local prince, quickly catches on to this and sees its huge potential. He eventually changes his name to Rothschild.

He has five sons whom he sends out across Europe to establish banks, one in each chosen country: England, France, Italy, Germany and Austria. Here they become the "king's bank", or what we now call, a central bank.

The first central bank to be established was the Bank of England. Instead of lending the English King gold bullion to be used for paying for war efforts, they demand the right, and only them, to issue paper receipts representing that gold. (paper money)

The King's loan is to run at 8% interest *for eternity*, paid in gold. No need to pay the principal, because Rothschild, in his turn, borrowed gold certificates at an interest of 2-4% per year.

The only limit to their banking profits is the King's or other King's need to borrow money. The more money they need to borrow the better. With a spread of 4-6% per year this action has a HUGE potential.

Now, with his five sons firmly established in the important corners of Europe, the best way to make money is *to make sure that the kings go to war* against each other, *and finance all their wars.* The bankers win either way all the time.

Napoleon

What better person to support for that end, than Napoleon? A small guy with huge ego, and world wide ambitions. The Napoleonic wars really got the Rothschild's started. For example, the Battle of Waterloo.

Thanks to their superior network of communication, they knew before anybody else who won that war, and that knowledge alone, put them in place to takeover the financial markets of their day.

The players knew to watch what Rothschild was doing, which he used to his full advantage. First sell — to get the avalanche going, — and when the flock is in full panic mode, selling at any price, he quietly bought it all, at rock bottom prices. That is how he played the London financial market on that last day of the Battle of Waterloo.

He absolutely took over the Bank of England.

In addition to that, all of the various Kings involved had to pay him interest on their loans. From then on, the rest is history, on how he managed to establish himself as the Key player in the distribution of funds throughout the western world — and later throughout the *rest of the world* to boot.

They don't necessarily own the funds and assets, but they control the main banks, and the chain that *distributes* these assets.

The Bank of China and Bank of Japan were also eventually established by Asian counterparts.

In an agreement signed in 1857 all Asian territories

agreed to have the Bank of England oversee and control all macro banking aspects in their territories. And that agreement still stands today.

Today, 5 out of the 7 central banks in the G7 group are controlled by Rothschild interests.

The FED

The last "central bank" to be established was the Federal Reserve Bank in America. The Americans resisted the idea of a central bank for the longest time, and it took a banking crisis, together with some long term political games, to get them to finally accept the idea, under the Federal Reserve Act in 1913. It has since been rightfully called "the crime of the (20th) century."

The Chinese Royal family, tracing its roots back to Genghis Khan, always had close ties with their Indonesian relatives. When mainland China went through its upheavals, during Mao, their assets were moved first to Taiwan; later to Jawa Tengah in Indonesia.

The same goes for The Shah of Iran. His main assets were also held and safeguarded there after the 1950's.

900-1000 A.D.

High Priests in Jawa Tengah get directions from God to travel to Bali (Little Jawa) and establish a Colony there.

Their first attempt failed so they returned.

Some 100 years later they received a second command from God to do the same. God gave directions for three nails to be nailed down, gold, silver, and bronze, and a Temple to be established. This time they succeed.

By 1500, the Royal courts of Solo moved there to safeguard the traditions and culture from the pressures of Islam taking over Jawa Tengah.

Further exploration and people go east. There are really interesting linguistic and cultural traces pointing to close contacts between Jawa/Bali and Polynesian, Mayan and Native Americans. Native American names and traditions can be found in Indonesia as well.

Illuminati breeding program — 1200-1300 A.D.

Queen Roro Kidul, a beautiful girl, marries the king of Solo. It is said that she shines, lighting up the room, and never grows old. ... that a special Being promised to always protect the Kingdom and return when needed. Her bloodline continues with a last name of Chakra Ningrat, meaning: "the illuminated".

1300 -1700 A.D.

Royals marry Royals and none other. The Jawa bloodline was important, and Chinese Royals and Middle Eastern Royals all intermarry.

In 1700 all major wars are basically between close or distant Royal family members. They are all related in one way or other. They fight over land and wealth. With advancing technology wars get more and more destructive and in an "enlightened" moment some agree to try, and systematically do something about it.

The Napoleonic war in Europe made a good reason to stop interfamily fighting.

Around 1750, 128 of the most important Royals agree to a "Breeding" plan. They marry or have children systematically, having their respective first son/daughter mate according to this same plan.

Their Objective

To engender the "King of Kings" : "The Enlightened One" : ... one King to represent each of the 128 Royal families of the world. Over the course of 7 generations they slowly bring their numbers down from 128 to 64; to 32; to 16; to 8; to 4; to 2; to 1.

Finally in the year 1900, "The One" is born. Now they have ONE individual who can honestly say, "I represent ALL of YOU." Let's call him "M1", short for "Monetary1".

The "King of Kings".

The 1920's recall

With M1 in existence it was time to move on to the next step in the plan.

In 1920-21, they started to consolidate (call in) their combined wealth, with the intention of placing it into the hands of M1.

M1 was to then redistribute the combined wealth of the world according to an agreed upon plan.

Nine of the most prominent Royal families were driving

this project, representing different regions of the world.

Together with the Chinese Royal KS, one of the most active and respected among them was PB.X (Paku Bueno X); M1's biological father and King of Solo from the "Chaka Ningrat", or "The illuminated", Solomon bloodline.

So in 1928, PB.X called a meeting in Solo, Jawa Tengah, for all the Families to attend. Here they sign a POA (Power of Attorney), transferring all their combined assets into the M1's hands. He was then supposed to distribute this wealth according to an agreed upon plan called, "The Plan of the Experts".

The Plan of the Experts - How it was supposed to work out according to "The Plan of the Experts" of 1928

The Plan of the Experts is thought to be divine. It is driven by a genuine attempt to better the fate of all mankind. To bring them into a material level of comfort, after which they are freed from daily troubles, to pursue man's ultimate goal of Unity with God, and with each and everyone.

It is a long worked upon plan of unifying the World, *"As good as possible; for as many as possible"* is their basic guiding principle.

If you have all the money in the world and you want to *"make the world a better place"* and a more equal world, how would you go about it?

This is a serious question.

The people faced with that problem, that opportunity, planned it along these lines all with very good intensions.

First collect the world's gold into one big pot. Set someone you trust in charge, but have checks and balances in place.

One of the primary objectives was to free the nations from Colonialism. These new nations should be governed as Guided democracies.

Up on top of the world power pyramid there should be a forum where every nation has a voice and a vote. Then, when ready, M1 would transfer his power to that world government body.

It was called "The United Nations".

All these new & old independent nations need financing. To supply that and track all major fund movements you need a Central bank to all the central banks.

Hence the BIS

The Bank of International Settlements in Switzerland was planned to be set up for that purpose. To give everybody access to the best and the brightest people regarding infrastructure, and the World Bank was incorporated for financing.

The WB job is to employ the best in their fields who then plan projects and infrastructure solutions around the world. They will also finance projects that cannot meet normal commercial bank requirements.

They are to approve cash utilizations from FED and other Banks. Your project needs a WB approval to get financed.

To feed the private side of world finance with cash you need an outlet. The FED was to take this role. It was to be the "cash cow" of the world, on the private side of banking.

The Fed was to supply all the "prime banks" with funding. The top 25 around the world. Not just American banks, but all others as well.

Here is where it all started to go wrong. The FED became a political tool for powerful agendas. Its owners eventually high jacked the system as a whole.

To help failing economies and guide them along they needed the IMF (International Monetary Fund). Their work was to be the lender of last resort. "We will help you — but…"

Here is where "Guided" democracy comes into play. All *the new small independent nations* that were planned, would at times run into financial trouble, and the IMF was supposed to be there to help straighten things out.

Justice

To solve international legal cases and humanitarian issues across National borders they needed an International court of Justice.

The Hague fills that role. One of its offsprings is the Geneva Conventions.

Later in the scheme once the new nations are firmly established and functional they can be joined into bigger blocks. All for the purpose of unity, peace, and togetherness.

The USA could stand as a good example, and similar solutions were foreseen for Europe, Africa, and Asia, as well.

These projects are still on the drawing board and if you study today's news you can see how the seeds are still there.

Just as with the EU, it is quietly there until suddenly the time is right, then things will move very fast.

The difference from what was originally planned and not, is that *other forces are now pushing the same agenda for control.*

These are very approximate time lines. Time will tell when it all will happen and how it will be implemented. At the present, there is a fight for control going on. As it stands today, we will end up with one of two solutions.

(1) A world paper currency backed by gold governed by a multinational assembly.

(2) A cashless society solution where ultimately the Banks, or their owners, control the money flows and supply.

The Objective

- Break Down Colonialism;
- Free the Nations and create an equal start;
- Control the New Nations through debt;
- Unify the World;
- *"As good as possible; for as many as possible."*
- Through a freedom War and economic stress on the colonial powers.

The US will be the first country to get access to big funding according to the "Plan of the Experts."

The FED borrows huge amounts of money and funds "the new deal" in the 1930's. The US is set to be the great liberator of nations and the "champion of democracy". To achieve this, the intention is for the US to;

- Build up the military;
- Function as world Police;
- Control the outcome of the future WWII.

WWII, Freed the Nations; Created Bases for the EU; and Created Bases for the UN.

In 1946 Three "Marshall" plans are set up within the UN to fund the world after WWII to free the nations and create an equal start, for Europe, Africa, and Asia . . .

. . . creating the need for a new way to create cash, only partly based on gold, hence the Breton Woods Conference, 1942-43 . . .

. . . leading to hyper accounts (a trading system within the FED that creates money out of nothing. Checks and balances do apply) . . .

. . . leading to more POWER to the FED/BoE/BIS banking power triangle, at the cost of the people controlling the gold / M1 (opening the door for the 1963-5 complete banking takeover of the monetary supply system)

WWII gets everybody into huge debts . . . leading to a Guided Democracy (instead of a Constitutional Republic).

Bandung Conference, 1955. M1 issues certificates to Africa and Asia.

But the FED/BoE/BIS never follow through!

The SPLIT between the Indonesians and the Chinese that started in 1928, that was triggered in 1934 by the death of PB.X, widens, and M1 looks to the USA and JFK for help to lessen the FED's POWER in the world.

JFK's and M1's shared Idea, — 3 agreements:

• Tampak Siring (Bali)
• Washington agreement
• "Green Hilton Memorial"

M1 transfers 140,000,000 kg of gold to JFK to back a New USD issued by US treasury (EO.11110, July 1963).

The objective is to replace the FED with the US

Treasury as the issuer of US dollars. Signed on November 14, 1963.

A few days later, on November 22nd, JFK is killed.

1964: M1 gives key speech "to build the world anew". He wants to start from scratch with a new UN, a new FED, a new money system, etc.

M1 is removed from power by a CIA supported coupe. He is held in house arrest until his death.

So how have they been able to pursue an agenda over many generations???

- They are very cleverly organized.

- The Visible power structure we see in the news is only part of it. At the top of each "little" pyramid sits people who were carefully selected and groomed. They don't end up there by accident and they don't have anywhere near the full picture.

- There is also the internal conflict within the system pushing for different agendas to consider.

- The visible power structure is comprised of the UN, the IMF, the WB, the EU, the FED, the BIS.

- The personal organization (Free Masonry) is built exactly the same way: 33 official degrees followed by 7 more official layers of superiority.

- 555 Top people in the bottom structure make up the base for the next level.

These people will work on many political systems & modules. Experiments like the Russian Communist system as well as the USA free market system was and is discussed and contemplated here. Let's see what works?

Both are now deemed failures with adjustments to EU being the middle way.

• The very Top level consists of just 16 people total. They control the finances and distribution of funds throughout the system. They issue and lend out gold backed paper certificates. Terms are usually no more than 33 years and interest of 2-3% per year payable in gold.

The underlying physical Gold assets are safeguarded by a second group not mentioned here.

A third group functions as controllers. They can block any movements of funds that do not meet the agreed upon plan.

To push movements and agendas you need the right people in the right places with the right intentions.

There are many ways to find and groom them. Listed below are a few. You can be assured that most if not all people who end up in these positions of power were at some point picked, regardless of whether or not they themselves realize it. Then to help "their" people get the job done they will always fall back to a very effective method:

Create the PROBLEM - Present the SOLUTION

This is how the masses are pushed along.

These 16 top people were removed by Banker backed hardliners around 1965-1968. Since then *the system has been high jacked.*

It is being utilized for gaining more and more personal power and control over the natural resources and industrial assets of the planet and the world.

A raping of the planet has occurred since, for the benefit of a very few, whose ultimate goal is ultimate control of the world.

The first visible attempt by Bankers to highjack the system was in 1910 when the **Jekyll Island Treaty** created the seed of what later became the **FED.**

How it has been USED since 1965 when the banking cartel took control and hijacked it all

So here is how it works.

For any Macro funds to move within the Banking system, the BoE, The FED and the BIS have to sign off.

The Vatican Bank is an unofficial record keeper, and as such, has a big stake in the game.

The BoE actually owns the FED (or the majority share) and the FED can do nothing without its OK.

The FED funds all the Prime Banks in the world such as Amro, HSBC, Citibank, etc.

These Prime Banks will then lend to various corporations around the world. Especially targeting the multinationals. They can be grouped together in areas of interest and it doesn't really matter where they originate from, because ultimately their source of funds is the same

What few people realize is that the FED also OWNS huge foundations that will invest directly into the same multinationals.

In the financial world these foundations will be perceived as being created by institutional money.

So through two separate legs they have a say, and benefit from anything that happens among these corporations.

The BoE/FED also have the inside view of what is required to be able to utilize the huge M1 funds that were set up in 1946, to rebuild the world. Now they can go to work and start utilizing those funds.

It is now very easy to understand how people like John F. Kennedy and his brother Robert saw it as their mission to warn the world of this dark and growing power.

They called it **"The Industrial/Military complex"** (TIMC) who they perceived is out to take over control of the USA and the world.

They did the best they could to limit its reach, and both statesmen paid the ultimate price for it.

So the Banks were left to systematically lend out money to regimes they knew would squander the loans on products their companies could provide.

The intention was to make sure these countries ended up with debts that they never could repay.

Only corrupt and/or military dictators need apply.

Funds set aside in 1946 for rebuilding the world, now end up in the pockets of the owners of multinational corporations.

In reality the money borrowed by these nations never leaves Washington, DC. They just move from one account to the next, leaving a lot of third world nations with huge debts.

Read the book *"Confessions of an Economic Hitman"* by John Perkins, for an inside view.

20-30 years later: Military regimes are replaced by democratic regimes wanting to do the right thing. They cannot repay these debts and, hat in hand, approach the banks with *"what can we do?"*

After some crises and mulling somebody presents the concept of **"swaps".**

That means multinationals will bid for and buy anything that is worth anything in that country, but pay the bank for it, instead of the country being fleeced.

Again, money never leaves Washington, but is just shifted from account to account, by it all;

- Mineral rights
- Oil rights
- Logging rights
- etc.

Everything of value in these countries is now owned by Multinational corporations. All of which are ultimately owned and controlled by the owners of the BoE/FED.

By using a "system" where they create money out of nothing, to lend out with interest, they now OWN the world — but they still want more, — TOTAL CONTROL.

Very simplified, you can divide today's controllers of the "system" into **hardliners** and **softliners**.

Regardless, here are some things they agree on.

This is a partial list of the **objective values of SOME people now running the world:**

• The Jewish people and their beliefs have to go!
• The Aryans are "the chosen ones" — Population control (target 1-1.5 B);
• The Garden of Eden is wrongly perceived;
• Lucifer wants to help Humanity and not keep Humanity in the dark;
• Lucifer is the bringer of enlightenment.
Hardliners who knew about the coming "freedom" War (WWII) used that knowledge to set up and educate Hitler.

The war was unavoidable but it could have played out very differently. German Industrialists connected to a secret University society called the Thule Society, picked out, supported, and educated Hitler. He was their man and their product.

A copy of the Thule society in America can be found at Yale. It's called Scull & Bones. Note how the German connections to the ex president Bush family runs for generations through these secret societies.

George W. Bush's grandfather was taken to court, in his day, for supplying materials and financing Hitler, while America was still at war with him.

It is amazing to find in today's world, that Hitler's values and goals are still very much alive, among the very top levels of our societies. But it is quite understandable when you realize that Hitler did not create those values but learned them from his Masters. Those Masters are still around, but in different form.

One common value is the belief that the world can only sustain 1-1.5 Billion people. That the Earth cannot handle any more than this, they claim. That means that **4.5 –5 billion of us will have to go.** But HOW, is where they get divided into *hardliners* versus *softliners.*

Hardliners will say things like "Anyway possible, it just needs to be quick or we will end up like another Atlantis"; "Let God decide who lives or dies, but whatever *WE* decide is OK by him, since otherwise He would not have placed us in this position of Power". A scary argument if there ever was one.

Softliners will say things like "We agree on the Goal, but we can reach it through Education and togetherness, etc. It will take time but we can get there eventually".

Recently softliners within the system have reached out to the "old gold" People (who have stayed underground since '65) to try and reign in the worst of the hardliner elements.

The gold people have had no say for a long time but Banks still have "old gold" certificates ticking at interest payable in gold in their vaults as funds.

And that's Leverage!

Shadows "Within the SYSTEM"

Within this old "gold standar" system there are checks and controls in place.

The controls are built as triangles where the 3 parties should not know or have direct contact with each other. This formula is repeated throughout the system on all levels.

The Banking cartel probably thought they could highjack the system for good, once they got the Fiat currency system — paper money with just faith backing it — fully in place and accepted by all. That gradual process was finalized when Nixon effectively took the USD off its tie to gold.

The Banking world seems to have miscalculated the strength of the control systems and are only now coming to the realization that they will need the cooperation of the gold people if they are to exist. That is why in the future we will see a shift in focus of funds from the West towards Asia, and eventually Africa.

The M1 position is on one of these three points.

• M1 acts as Holder (H) of the assets. He will act as the front face of the owner but actually does not have anything to do with owning the underlying hard assets. It is a management position.

• The accounts will be in his name and he signs for a lot of it. He has the right to 2.5 % (basically the interest) of the funds under his management.

• He is supported by a team of 70 people, directly beneath him.

On the opposite side of M1, at the base of the triangle, are the OWNERS (OW) of the hard assets.

They will sit on and control the underlying physical assets. These are the assets that were "legalized".

Legalized means that a company came and inspected the asset and issued a certificate based on said asset. Now, the certificate can easily be moved and lent out at interest, while the underlying asset never has to be touched.

This certainly makes Banking a whole lot easier. No need to cart 1,000's of tons of gold around.

The third top level is that of the Controller (C). The ultimate green light for the use of any asset. He can stop anything the others decide on, but rarely instigates macro fund movements.

It seems the Chinese Royals (KS) kept this part within their bloodline. All three (H,OW,C) signatories are required for utilization of any given asset. The same controller (C) can sign for hundreds of different accounts and their position code within the system is 3/3/3.

Another position code within the system is 6/6/6 which is one of higher authority than 3/3/3. At this point in time that Master Power of Attorney paper is still waiting for a name to be filled in.

The 'old gold' people also talk of these code positions as periods.

Supposedly the 6/6/6 "period" is to be a transition period leading into a 9/9/9 period of ultimate peace and happiness on earth.

They in turn get their information and prophecies from, among other things, an ancient "Gold book" that contains everything from beginning to end of the human drama on earth. It is believed to be part of what King Solomon left here, together with his sword. It can only be read by selected priests using a specific tool.

Visible Power Structure

Freemasons

The Freemasons, which are basically the more visible part of the Templar Knights, are built up much the same way as the rest of the "system".

The visible base has 33 levels, and you think you are at the top if you reach 33 degree Mason.

They do a lot of good around the world and are a serious player in allocating funds for various projects. It is unclear, though, what or who is actually at the very top and the spirit they worship.

Invisible Power Structure

Above the 33 degree Mason there are again 7 more layers leading to the ultimate "King of Kings".

At this level there is a lot of work with Spirit. All profess to be working for God, but perceptions of God will vary.

Some will say it's Christ that should sit at the top; others claim that Lucifer is the good One.

If the top is Good, the rest follows, but if the top is Bad, the same goes as well.

Time will tell who ultimately takes the throne on a permanent basis.

What's next?

There seems to be two ways this can go depending who ends up winning the current struggle for control over the "system" (or a compromise including bits of both).

• The "gold" people come back into the game. This means we come back on some sort of gold standard with an international currency controlled by a multinational assembly of sorts; more funds available for developing regions.

• The "Bankers" continue to rule. A full on Fiat currency system using a cashless society model. All transactions having to go through a bank, leaving them in 100% control. This will be perceived as having a lot of advantages. No more theft, terrorists, drugs and such illegal activities.

They will know everything there is about you. You will be paying all your taxes automatically, whatever they are set to be, and if you, for any reason, do not follow what THEY perceive is the right track, they will cut you off.

You will not be able to buy and sell.

With no access to money or markets there is nowhere to hide. At first you will still have your plastic card, but that would soon be replaced by the implanted and much more personal chip, that they are now testing in different places around the world.

Either way, rest assured, our economic system will first have to fail. It is still the old proven method:

Create the problem - Present the solution.

What to do?

Go back to basics. Live your life as a sovereign being. One who has the opportunity to decide for him/herself what one should do in any given situation. Like the early pioneers of America. To do that you need to:

• Have land and housing you can call your own. No loans or obligations to any banks.

• Control your own food and water supply. If you can't grow it, store it! A three year supply of essentials will go a long way towards taking care of whatever may come in the future.

• Surround yourself with like minded people, and enjoy life as it unfolds.

Whatever we have ahead of us is just like birth pains, ultimately leading to the next step in the human drama, with us living life in harmony with the universe, and closer to God, and our full human potential.

Enjoy your journey home!

2
Conclusions

Why are the Templars Suddenly Being Attacked? WHY NOW? - Could it be that they have deposed the ruling Elite? (By Rayelan, www.rumormillnews.com)

When the Elite has an enemy, the normal practice is to destroy that enemy. If they can't do it quickly by killing him, then they do it slowly by either bankrupting him, framing him for crimes and jailing him, or destroying his reputation.

In the case of the modern day Templars... they are carefully hidden... usually in plain sight... or the higher ranking ones... deep below the earth in underground installations that the elite DARE not breech.

Because of this, the Elite can't destroy them in the normal way so they have to destroy their reputation.

As for my question in the article below... Is Obama a Reverse Trojan or is he the Jewish Messiah? I don't have the answer. For all I know... the Barack Obama who was created by the Templars... to be a Reverse Trojan Horse... could have been replaced by an Elite clone... or he could have been altered.

Notice photos of him with surgery scars evident on his neck and head? You can see before and after photos of his neck and see that the scars were NOT there in earlier photos two weeks before.

See both photos here. http://tinyurl.com/6d2vzcd

There has always been an opposition to the Elite who rule the world at the moment. This opposition has always been in secret societies... and the only society we know about are the Knights Templar.

Note this article about Barack Obama: *"Is Barack Obama the JEWISH Messiah? Was he a REVERSE TROJAN HORSE"* (in the 2008 Election)?

http://tinyurl.com/68dstbw

Let's put together the pieces of the puzzle.

We're going to lay things out... we have NO idea if any of this is true... and no idea of what will happen to Barack Obama if suddenly everyone realizes that he's NOT what people think he is... but in fact... he's much more!! That he's the ultimate end of a breeding experiment.

RMNews - 06.16.2009 - Freedom, CA. Posted By: Rayelan.

Shortly before the 2008 election, one of my sources told me that Obama is a "reverse trojan horse."

I rolled this around for months. I could see him as a Muslim in Christian's clothing... i.e. a TROJAN HORSE... but I couldn't see him as a "reverse Trojan." I could not figure out what he was "reversing" — until today. I woke up realizing that...

Rumors on the Internet, some from FOIA reports, have stated that:

1. Barack Obama is from the African mystery schools.

What are those? Those are centers of higher learning that have existed in Africa since the beginning of time. JFK, Jr. knew about them, and the deal he made with Pope John Paul II, to become President, would allow him to pick the next pope. I believe he would have chosen Cardinal Arinze.

2. Rumors say that Obama's parents are not his real parents.

His real parents are from the Egyptian Royal family, and the King David bloodline, probably through **Emperor Haile Selassie** who can trace an unbroken bloodline to King Solomon... son of King David.

3. Rumors... which I think come from FOIA searches... say that Obama's grandfather, Stanley Dunham was a spy for the German **Abwehr** during WWII.

Admiral Wilhelm Canaris headed the Abwehr during WWII, and according to my late husband, Gunther; Canaris also headed the Knights Templars.

Also according to Gunther, and to other Templars I met while in Austria, the Templars are the true royal bloodline on earth. They come from the descendants of the House of David who were exiled in 70 AD when the Romans obliterated King Solomon's temple.

According to Gunther, the bloodline of the House of David traveled all over the world and the true royal families... worldwide... have a bloodline that traces back to

King David.

There was a secret society that existed before the Templars. I do not know what they called themselves... but they passed their information orally on to the next generation... all the way up until the year AD 938, when on a rain swept, desolate day, at Larambique, in the foot hills of the massive Mt. Blanc, a group of dedicated monks and their worldly brothers gathered to form a new Order to keep alive the words which God had granted Solomon, in a dream.

"Each living being possesses basic divine rights. The most basic right is the right of self determination. Each and every being upon Earth is divinely given the right to control his own life. Other inalienable* divinely granted rights include food, shelter, clothing and fair compensation for work well done."

http://tinyurl.com/6eaaxbc

The Templars started pilgrimages to the Holy Lands where they built the stable for their horses OVER King Solomon's Temple.

They did this because they knew that there was a treasure far greater than gold and jewels, in Solomon's Temple. They knew that there was a library there that was **a duplicate of the Library at Alexandria, plus the Tibetan libraries.**

Remember, Admiral Canaris was a Templar and a descendant of the House of David. Realize that no one could become a Templar unless he could trace his bloodline to the House of David. **This is the piece of information that the Templar researchers are missing.** With this piece of the puzzle, many of the other things now make sense.

Remember...

It started with King Solomon, in Jerusalem, around 930 B.C. Solomon was a very successful King who amassed huge wealth ... especially gold.

He had 600 wives & concubines and thousands of children.

Knowing that his country would fall apart after his death, he selected one of his most trusted wives, Queen Shaba, or Balquish, to protect his assets, bloodline, and traditions thereafter.

Sometime later, she leaves Jerusalem taking everything back to where she came from: Java.

There she establishes the Courts of what later become known as Solo Jawa ... there safeguarding the gold assets, King Solomon's bloodline, and the religious traditions of his court.

snip

The Royal Solo family ties expand to include the Chinese Royals.

Gunther was descended from the Hungarian Esterhaszy who trace its bloodline to Ghengis Khan... and on to Kublai Khan (1215-1294), last Khan of the Mongol Empire and Emperor of China.

Keep in mind, that this analysis may be leaving out pieces of the puzzle. We only know what we picked up by being a fly on the wall at many meetings Gunther had with the Templars, and with members of Faction Two, which was started by Templars but now contains freedom loving people from every country in the world..

Also... remember others are helping me put this puzzle together. Without input from knowledgeable people, we may never know the entire truth.

Khan... as in Ghengis Khan... is a title... very similar to the Jewish word Cohen, which is now a last name. Cohens are descended from the priest class.

Now look at this...

• Negudar, Mongol General who converted to Islam and took name of Ahmad Khan.

• Khan Asparukh, founder of modern-day Bulgaria.

• Aga Khan, the hereditary title of the Imam of the Niza-ri- Muslims.

• Aga Khan IV, title of Kari-m al-Hussayni- KBE CC GCC, the current Aga Khan.

The Aga Khan IV is the man who we were told would be the leader of the Muslim Califate once it rises all around the world.

Continuing from above:

1000 A.D.

A few "Knights" spend 9 years in Jerusalem digging out the ruins of King Solomon's Temple.

They discover something that makes them very powerful once they return to Europe.

They get special privileges from the Pope. This leads to The Knights Templar Order being established with direct access to the Pope.

• The Knights Templar quickly become Europe's protector of wealth, and of the pilgrims traveling to Jerusalem.

• This leads to the establishment of the first Banking system, working throughout the European world.

• People of means deposit their wealth with the Knights Templar and then draw from it when they are in the "Holy Land" or on the road back home.

1064 A.D.

• The Knights Templar first establish a connection with the old King Solomon bloodline in Solo Jawa.

• They discover something that makes them very powerful once back in Europe.

What did they discover? Gunther and other Templars told me that, along with tonnes of King Solomon's gold, were books, scrolls and discs that were taken back to the salt mines near Salzburg, Austria. That location was chosen for the library because they believed it would best preserve the books.

Friday the 13th, October, 1307.

The Templars are now rich, powerful, and independent from European church and state organizations.

The French King, together with the Pope, conspires to confiscate their assets and destroy their power. All over Europe, on Friday the 13th, October, 1307, the Templars are hunted down, jailed, and many are killed, and their land holdings and assets are confiscated.

The Templars hide and flee in three main directions.

One group flees into the mountains of central Europe to what eventually becomes Switzerland.

One group flees north and establishes a safe haven in northern Scotland, and in Scandinavia, while the third group flees west to Portugal, from where they eventually migrate to America.

I have skipped a number of pages in the pdf - (on which this book is based). You can view it at this link...

http://www.rumormillnews.com/pdfs/HistoryofMoney.pdf

The Chinese Royal family, tracing its roots back to Djengis Kahn, always had very close ties with their Indonesian relatives.

When mainland China goes through its upheavals during Mao their assets are moved first to Taiwan, later to Indonesia.

The same goes for The Shah of Iran. His main assets are also held and safeguarded there after 1950's.

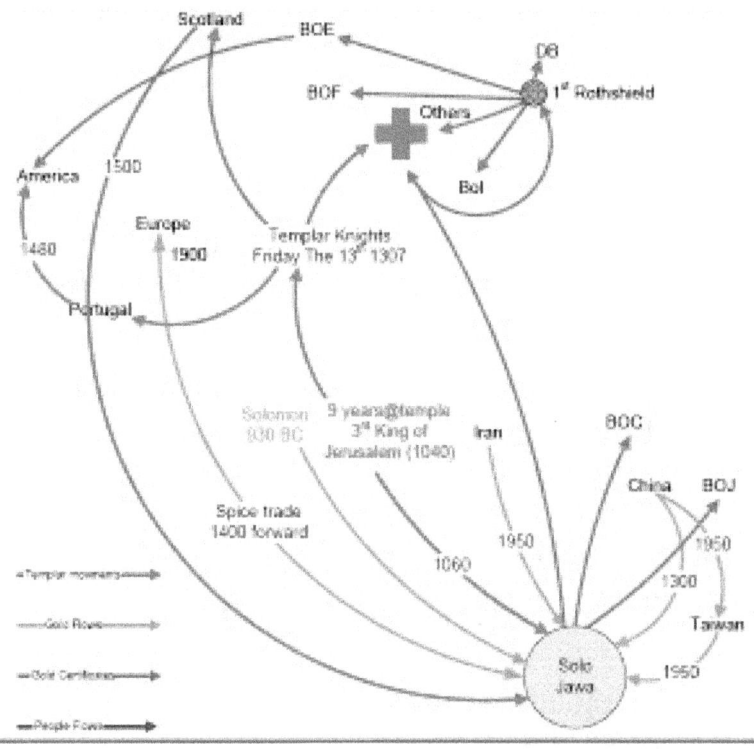

I have skipped another large portion of the document.

Illuminatl breeding program — 1200-1300 A.D.

Queen Roro Kidul, a beautiful girl, marries the king of Solo. It is said that she shines, lighting up the room, and never grows old. ... that a special Being promised to always protect the Kingdom and return when needed. Her bloodline continues with a last name of Chakra Ningrat, meaning: "the illuminated".

128 Royal Families start a "breeding program".

Who are these royals? Are they the SAME royals who make up the sitting royals world wide? In some cases, Yes. In some cases, No. And I don't have all the answers, so you will have to wait until I find those answers.

1300 -1700 A.D.

Royals marry Royals and none other. The Jawa bloodline was important, and Chinese Royals and Middle Eastern Royals all intermarry.

In 1700 all major wars are basically between close or distant Royal family members. They are all related in one way or other. They fight over land and wealth. With advancing technology wars get more and more destructive and in an "enlightened" moment some agree to try, and systematically do something about it.

Their Objective: *Create the "King of Kings", "the enlightened one"*

A person who would equally represent each and every one of the participating 128 Royal families of the world.

Over the course of 7 generations they slowly bring down the number of Royal families from 128 families to one (128/2=64/2=32/2=16/2=8/2=4/2=2/2=1).

Finally in the year 1900, "The One" is born. Now they have ONE individual who can honestly say, "I represent ALL of YOU." Let's call him "M1". Short for "Monetary1".

The "King of Kings".

This is where the dark, evil and greedy side of the illuminati, as we know it today, hijacked the plan.

[Continuing from the information above]

The 1920's recall

With M1 in existence it was time to move on to the next step in the Plan.

In 1920-21, they started to consolidate (call in) their combined wealth, with the intention of placing it into the hands of M1.

M1 was to then redistribute the combined wealth of the world according to an agreed upon plan.

Nine of the most prominent Royal families representing different regions of the world were driving this project. Together with the Chinese Royal "KS", one of the most active and respected among them were PB X (paku Bueno X). M1's biological father and the king of Solo from the "Chaka Ningrat" or "The illuminated" Solomon bloodline.

Here is where it started to go wrong; the FED became a political tool to push power agendas. Its owners eventually high jacked the whole system.

The Objective

- Break Down Colonialism;
- Free the Nations and create an equal start;
- Control the New Nations through debt;
- Unify the World;

- ***"As good as possible; for as many as possible."***
- Through a freedom War and economic stress on the colonial powers.

I am going to stop quoting the pdf file here because I have given you the background you need to be able to see where I am going with my analysis.

... If all the royal families in the world are blood related and they all come from the House of David, which I have been writing about since 1994, and...

... **If there was a Templar breeding plan, then all the royal families bred with Templars.**

Admiral Canaris was a Templar. According to a document on the Internet... one that was meant to discredit Obama, his grandfather worked for the German Abwehr as a spy during WWII.

In my opinion, **the Abwehr were the good Germans who were trying to put an end to Hitler, before the Illuminati from the City of London** (the ones who hijacked the plan) **bombed Germany and Austria back into the stone age.**

If Stanley Dunham was an **Abwehr**... aka, **Faction Two operative**... then he would have done as he was told. If he were ordered to marry his daughter off to a black man and have them pretend to be the parents of Barack Obama, he would have done that . . .

. . . **a member of Faction Two doesn't question orders . . . he does as he is told.**

According to a source... who had nothing to do with the creation of the document I have been quoting from... M1 was kept under house arrest until his death in 1950.

If our hunch is correct, Barack Obama was created by the Abwehr to replace M1.

If we are right, we will soon find out that his bloodline connects all they way back to the House of David, and to the long line of Jewish Kings.

I do NOT know how this information will surface. Maybe in a court case where he has to prove that he is a natural born citizen.

Maybe the documents that will unfold as he tries to prove he is a natural born citizen will actually prove that he is the Jewish Messiah!!

Jews do not believe that the Messiah will be divine. A fundamental difference between Judaism and Christianity is the Jewish conviction that God is so different from humanity that he could never become a human.

The Messianic Age

When the Messiah does come, he will inaugurate the messianic age (sometimes called the **Olam Ha-Ba**, World to Come). The **Tanakh** employs the following descriptions about this period:

- Peace among all nations (Isaiah 2:4; Micah 4:3);

- Perfect harmony and abundance in nature (Isaiah 11:6-9) (but some interpret this as an allegory for peace and prosperity);

• All Jews return from exile to Israel (Isaiah 11:11-12; Jeremiah 23:8; 30:3; Hosea 3:4-5);

• Universal acceptance of the Jewish God and Jewish religion (Isaiah 2:3; 11:10; 66:23; Micah 4:2-3; Zechariah 14:9);

• No sin or evil; all Israel will obey the commandments (Zephaniah 3:13; Ezekiel 37:24);

• Reinstatement of the Temple (Ezekiel 37:26-27).

Ezekiel 37:24-28 sums up many of the requirements:

*"**And David my servant shall be king over them;** and they shall all have one shepherd : they shall also walk in my judgments and observe my statutes, and do them. And they shall dwell in the land that I have given unto Jacob my servant, wherein your fathers have dwelt; and they shall dwell therein, even they, and their children, and their children's children for ever; and my servant David shall be their prince for ever.*

Moreover I will make a covenant of peace with them; it shall be an everlasting covenant with them; and I will place them, and multiply them, will set my sanctuary in the midst of them for evermore. My tabernacle also shall be with them: yea, I will be their God, and they shall be my people. And the [nations] shall know that I the Lord do sanctify Israel, when my sanctuary shall be in the midst of them for evermore."

The Jewish Messiah is called the **Olam Ha-Ba**, World to Come. Do you see the similarity to Obama's name?

http://tinyurl.com/38uxgu

We know that Barack Obama came from a Christian family... his grandparents and mother.

His father and step father were Muslim. He was raised Muslim for his first 10 years. He spent another 20 years in a Christian church.

At the moment, it looks as if Barack Obama is Israel's worst enemy — since Jimmy Carter, who barely escaped assassination recently in Palestine.

If Barack Obama is a reverse Trojan, we may see the restoration of the original plan that the History of World Banking lays out. He may throw the money changers out of the temple and restore lending to what Christians and Muslims have historically done... i.e. **NO USURY!!**

If President Obama is the real Jewish Messiah, he will have to educate all the people of the earth about the perversions that have taken place regarding **the 3 main religions**... ever since 70 AD.

The way the pieces of the puzzle now stand... they present President Barack Obama as a Trojan horse in reverse who knew he could only be elected by making his backers think he was a Muslim and a Communist to boot.

When his *true* bloodline is shown... maybe in a Supreme Court case... what will the world do?

Will it prove that he is a natural born citizen?

Or will it prove that he is the Jewish Messiah?

The Templars believe that they are descended from the House of David. Admiral Canaris was the last Templar Grand Master, as far as we know. Possibly his son has replaced him... or maybe Admiral Canaris is still alive!!

Gunther's father worked directly for Admiral Canaris during WWII... and evidently so did Stanley Dunham.

These are the facts as we know them today. With new information the picture may change.

[*Please remember that what we have re-released in this book, is possibly one of the most guarded stories on the planet right now.*]

Appendix

History of World Banking

Knights Templar Banking

Knights Templar Banking History

The Knights Templar Order became an extremely powerful entity during the Middle Ages. When a man joined the Knights Templar he took an oath of poverty and his wealth and lands were donated to the Knights Templar order.

The first donation of land was given to the Templars in 1127 by Count Thybaud of Champagne at Barbonne-Fayel, fifty kilometres north-west of Troyes. Further donations of money and land were given to the Knights Templar order by nobles and Kings.

The Knights Templar were also given certain privileges, for example, King Alfonso I of Spain granted the Knights Templar exemption of tax on a fifth of the wealth taken from the Moors. Various Popes also gave privileges to the order. The Knights Templar order therefore became extremely wealthy and became involved in Knights Templar Banking activities.

Knights Templar Banking - Usury (money lending)

The Knights Templar banking activities led to their involvement with Usury. Usury is a form of money lending where an initial charge is made for a loan, or interest is charged on the repayments. The increase of the Knights Templar wealth, in turn, led them to becoming involved in banking, which in turn brought even greater wealth into the Knights Templar order.

Their financial power due to their banking activities led to great political power in all of the countries in Europe of the Middle Ages.

Knights Templar Banking - the decline of the order

The Knights Templar banking activities increased their financial wealth and political power.

Powerful monarchs went to the Knights Templar treasurers to obtain loans to finance their interests which included financing the cost of mounting a war. This was the case of King Philip IV of France (1268-1314) who was already heavily in debt to the Knights Templar when he requested a further loan to finance a war.

The request was refused and a furious King Philip mounted an attack on the Knights Templar order.

Pope Clement V initiated enquiries into the order and thousands of Knights Templar were arrested across Europe on charges of heresy.

Anyone found sheltering a Templar was under threat of excommunication. This led to the decline of the Knights Templar Banking activities — and the order itself.

The Knights Templars
Part 1

The Knights Templars were the earliest founders of the military orders, and are the type on which the other military orders are modelled.

They are marked in history (1) by their humble beginning, (2) by their marvellous growth and (3) by their tragic end.

Their humble beginning

Right after the deliverance of Jerusalem from Moslem control, the Crusaders, considering their vow fulfilled, returned in a body to their homes, but the defense of this precarious conquest, surrounded as it was by Mohammedan neighbors, remained.

In 1118, during the reign of Baldwin II, Hugues de Payens, a knight of Champagne, and eight companions, bound themselves by a perpetual vow taken in the presence of the Patriarch of Jerusalem, to defend the Christian kingdom.

Baldwin accepted their services, and assigned them a portion of his palace, adjoining the temple of the city; hence their title *"pauvres chevaliers du temple"* (Poor Knights of the Temple).

Poor they were indeed, being reduced to living on alms, and so long as they were only nine, they were hardly prepared to render important services, unless it were as escorts to pilgrims on their way from Jerusalem to the banks of the Jordan River, then frequented as a place of devotion.

The Templars had as yet neither distinctive habit nor rule. Hugues de Payens journeyed to the west to seek the approbation of the Church and to obtain recruits.

At the Council of Troyes (1128), at which he assisted and at which St. Bernard was the leading spirit, the Knights Templars adopted the Rule of St. Benedict, as recently reformed by the Cistercians.

They accepted not only the three perpetual vows, besides the crusader's vow, but also the austere rules concerning the chapel, the refectory, and the dormitory. They also adopted the white habit of the Cistercians, adding to it a red cross.

Notwithstanding the austerity of the monastic rule, recruits flocked to the new order, which thenceforth comprised four ranks of brethren:

- the **knights**, equipped like the heavy cavalry of the Middle Ages;

- the **serjeants**, who formed the light cavalry;

And two ranks of non-fighting men:

- the **farmers**, entrusted with the administration of temporals; &

- the **chaplains**, who alone were vested with sacerdotal orders, to minister to the spiritual needs of the order.

The Templas' marvellous growth

The order owed its rapid growth in popularity to the fact that it combined the two great passions of the Middle Ages, **religious fervour** and **martial prowess**.

Even before the Templars had proved their worth, the ecclesiastical and lay authorities heaped on them favors of every kind, both spiritual and temporal.

The popes took them under their immediate protection, exempting them from all other jurisdiction, episcopal or secular. Their property was assimilated to the church estates and exempted from all taxation, even from the ecclesiastical tithes, while their churches and cemeteries could not be placed under interdict.

This soon brought about conflict with the clergy of the Holy Land, inasmuch as the increase of the landed property of the order led, owing to its exemption from tithes, to the diminution of the revenue of the churches. And the interdicts, at that time used and abused by the episcopate, became to a certain extent inoperative wherever the order had churches and chapels in which Divine worship was regularly held.

As early as 1156 the clergy of the Holy Land tried to restrain the exorbitant privileges of the military orders, but in Rome every objection was set aside, the result being a growing antipathy on the part of the secular clergy against these orders.

The temporal benefits which the order received from all the sovereigns of Europe were no less important. The Templars had **commanderies** in every state.

In France they formed no less than eleven **bailiwicks**, subdivided into more than forty-two **commanderies.** In Palestine it was for the most part with sword in hand that the Templars extended their possessions at the expense of the Mohammedans.

Their castles are still famous owing to the remarkable ruins which remain: **Safèd**, built in 1140; **Karak of the desert** (1143); and, most importantly of all, **Castle Pilgrim**, built in 1217 to command a strategic defile on the sea-coast.

In these castles, which were both monasteries and cavalry-barracks, the life of the Templars was full of contrasts. A contemporary describes the Templars as *"in turn lions of war and lambs at the hearth; rough knights on the battlefield, pious monks in the chapel; formidable to the enemies of Christ, gentleness itself towards His friends."* (Jacques de Vitry).

Having renounced all the pleasures of life, they faced death with a proud indifference; they were the first to attack, the last to retreat, always docile to the voice of their leader, the discipline of the monk being added to the discipline of the soldier.

As an army they were never very numerous.

A contemporary tells us that there were 400 knights in Jerusalem at the zenith of their prosperity; he does not give the number of serjeants, who were more numerous, but it was a picked body of men who, by their noble example, inspirited the remainder of the Christian forces.

They were thus the terror of the Mohammedans.

Were they defeated, it was upon them that the victor vented his fury, as they were forbidden to offer a ransom. When taken prisoners, they scornfully refused the freedom offered them on condition of apostasy.

At the siege of Safèd (1264), at which ninety Templars met death, eighty others were taken prisoner and refusing to deny Christ died martyrs to the Faith. This fidelity cost them dearly. It has been computed that in less than two centuries almost 20,000 Templars, both knights and serjeants, perished in war.

These frequent hecatombs rendered it difficult for the order to increase in numbers and also brought about a decline of the true crusading spirit.

As the order was compelled to make immediate use of the recruits, the original rule in Latin which required a probationary period, fell into disuse. Even excommunicants, who, as was the case with many crusaders, wished to expiate their sins, were admitted.

All that was required of a new member was a blind obedience, as imperative in the soldier as in the monk. He had to declare himself forever *"serf et esclave de la maison"* (French text of the rule).

To prove his sincerity, he was subjected to a secret test concerning the nature of which nothing has ever been discovered, although it gave rise to the most extraordinary accusations.

The great wealth of the order may also have contributed to a certain laxity in morals, but the most serious charge against it was its insupportable pride and love of power.

At the apogee of its prosperity, it was said to possess 9,000 estates. With its accumulated revenues it had amassed great wealth, which was deposited in its temples at London, England and Paris, France.

Numerous princes and private individuals had banked their personal property there, because of the uprightness and solid credit of such bankers. In Paris the royal treasure was kept in the Temple.

Quite independent, except from the distant authority of the pope, and possessing power equal to that of the leading temporal sovereigns, the order soon assumed the right to direct the weak and irresolute government of the Kingdom of Jerusalem, a feudal kingdom transmissible through women and exposed to all the disadvantages of minorities, regencies, and domestic discord.

However, the Templars were soon opposed by the Order of Hospitallers, which had in its turn become military, and was at first the imitator, and later the rival of the Templars.

This ill-timed interference of the orders in the Jerusalem government multiplied the rivalry and fights, and this at a time when the formidable power of Saladin threatened the very existence of the Latin Kingdom.

While the Templars sacrificed themselves with customary bravery, in this final struggle, they were, nevertheless, partly responsible for the downfall of Jerusalem.

To put an end to this baneful rivalry between the military orders, there was a very simple remedy at hand, namely their amalgamation.

This was officially proposed by St. Louis at the Council of Lyons, in 1274. It was proposed again in 1293 by Pope Nicholas IV, who called a general consultation of the Christian states on this point. This idea was canvassed by all the publicists of that time, who demand either a combining of the existing orders, or the creation of a third order to supplant them.

Never in fact had the question of the crusaders been more eagerly taken up than after their failure. As the grandson of St. Louis, Philip the Fair could not remain indifferent to these proposals for a crusade.

As the most powerful prince of his time, the direction of the movement belonged to him. To assume this direction, all he demanded was the necessary supplies of men and especially of money.

Such is the genesis of his campaign for the suppression of the Templars. It has been attributed wholly to his well-known cupidity. Even on this supposition he needed a pretext, for he could not, without sacrilege, lay hands on possessions that formed part of the ecclesiastical domain.

To justify such a course, the sanction of the Church was necessary, and this the king could only obtain by maintaining the sacred purpose for which the possessions were destined.

Admitting that he was sufficiently powerful to encroach upon the property of the Templars in France, he still needed the concurrence of the Church to secure control of their possessions in the other countries of Christendom.

Such was the purpose of the wily negotiations of this self-willed and cunning sovereign, and of his still more treacherous counsellors, with Clement V, a French pope of weak character and easily deceived.

The rumour that there had been a prearrangement between the king and the pope has been finally disposed of. A doubtful revelation, which allowed Philip to make the prosecution of the Templars as heretics a question of orthodoxy, affording him the opportunity which he desired to invoke the action of the Holy See.

The Templars' tragic end

In the trial of the Templars two phases must be seen: the *royal commission* and the *papal commission*.

First phase — the *royal* commission

Philip the Fair made a preliminary inquiry, and, on the strength of so-called revelations of a few unworthy and degraded members, secret orders were sent throughout France to arrest all the Templars on the same day (13 October, 1307) and to submit them to a most rigorous examination.

The king did this at the request of the ecclesiastical inquisitors, it was made to appear, but in reality without their co-operation.

In this inquiry, torture — the use of which was authorized by the cruel procedure of the age in the case of crimes committed without witnesses — was pitilessly employed.

Owing to the lack of evidence, the accused could only be convicted through their own confession, and to extort this confession, the use of torture was considered necessary and legitimate.

There was one feature in the organization of the order which gave rise to suspicion, namely the secrecy with which the rites of initiation were conducted. The secrecy is explained by the fact that the receptions always took place in a chapter, and the chapters, owing to the delicate and grave questions discussed, were, and had to be necessarily, held in secret.

An indiscretion in the matter of secrecy entailed exclusion from the order. The secrecy of these initiations, however, had two grave disadvantages.

As these receptions could take place wherever there was a **commandery**, they were carried on without publicity and were free from all surveillance or control from the higher authorities, the tests being entrusted to the discretion of subalterns who were often uncultivated and rough.

Under such conditions, it is not to be wondered at that abuses crept in. One need only recall what took place almost daily at the time in the brotherhoods of artisans, the initiation of a new member being too often made the occasion for a parody more or less sacrilegious of baptism, or of the Mass.

The second disadvantage of this secrecy was, that it gave an opportunity to the enemies of the Templars, and they were numerous, to infer from this mystery every conceivable malicious supposition, and base on it the monstrous imputations.

The Templars were accused of spitting upon the Cross, of denying Christ, of permitting sodomy, of worshipping an idol, all in the most impenetrable secrecy. Such were the Middle Ages, when prejudice was so vehement that, to destroy an adversary, men did not recoil from inventing the most criminal charges.

Most of the accused declared themselves guilty of these secret crimes after being subjected to such ferocious torture that many of them succumbed. Some made similar confessions *without* the use of torture, but through fear of it, the threat had been sufficient. Such was the case with the grand master himself, Jacques de Molay, who acknowledged later that he had lied to save his life.

Carried on without the authorization of the pope, who had the military orders under his jurisdiction, this investigation was radically corrupt both as to its intent and as to its procedure. Not only did Clement V enter an energetic protest, but he annulled the entire trial and suspended the powers of the bishops and their inquisitors.

However, the offense had been admitted and remained the irrevocable basis of the entire subsequent proceedings. Philip the Fair took advantage of the discovery to have the University of Paris bestow upon himself the title of Champion and Defender of the Faith, and to stir up public opinion at the States General of Tours against the heinous crimes of the Templars.

Moreover, he succeeded in having the confessions of the accused confirmed in presence of the pope by seventy-two Templars, who had been specially chosen and coached beforehand.

In view of this investigation at Poitiers (June, 1308), the pope, until then sceptical, at last became concerned and opened a new commission, the procedure of which he himself directed. He reserved the cause of the order to the papal commission, leaving individuals to be tried by the diocesan commissions to whom he restored their powers.

Second phase — the *papal* commission

The second phase of the process was the papal inquiry, which was not restricted to France, but extended to all the Christian countries of Europe, and even to the Orient.

In most of the other countries — Portugal, Spain, Germany, Cyprus — **the Templars were found innocent;** and in Italy, except for a few districts, the decision was the same. **But in France** the episcopal inquisitors, resuming their activities, took the facts as established at the trial, and confined themselves to reconciling the repentant guilty members, imposing various canonical penances, extending even to imprisonment for life.

Only those who persisted in heresy were to be turned over to the secular arm, but, by a rigid interpretation of this provision, those who had withdrawn their former confessions were considered relapsed heretics; thus fifty-four Templars who had recanted after having confessed were condemned as relapsed and publicly burned on 12 May, 1310.

Subsequently all the other Templars, who had been examined at the trial, with very few exceptions declared themselves guilty.

At the same time the papal commission, appointed to examine the cause of the order, had entered upon its duties and gathered together the documents which were to be submitted to the pope, and to the general council called to decide as to the final fate of the order.

The culpability of single persons, which was looked upon as established, did not involve the guilt of the order. Although the defense of the order was poorly conducted, it could not be proved that the order as a body professed any heretical doctrine, or that a secret rule, distinct from the official rule, was practised.

Consequently, at the General Council of Vienne in Dauphiné on 16 October, 1311, the majority were favorable to the maintenance of the order.

The pope, irresolute and harrassed, finally adopted a middle course: he decreed the dissolution, not the condemnation of the order, and not by penal sentence, but by an Apostolic Decree (Bull of 22 March, 1312).

The order having been suppressed, the pope himself was to decide as to the fate of its members and the disposal of its possessions. As to the property, it was turned over to the rival Order of Hospitallers to be applied to its original use, the defence of the Holy Places.

In Portugal, however, and in Aragon the possessions were vested in two new orders, the Order of Christ in Portugal and the Order of Montesa in Aragon.

As to the members, the Templars who were recognized guiltless, were allowed either to join another military order or to return to the secular state. In the latter case, a pension for life, charged to the possessions of the order, was granted them. On the other hand, the Templars who had pled guilty before their bishops were to be treated "according to the rigours of justice, tempered by a generous mercy".

The pope reserved to his own judgment the cause of the grand master and his three first dignitaries. They had confessed their guilt; it remained to reconcile them with the Church, after they had testified to their repentance with the customary solemnity.

To give this solemnity more publicity, a platform was erected in front of the Notre-Dame for the reading of the sentence. But at the supreme moment the grand master recovered his courage and proclaimed the innocence of the Templars and the falsity of his own alleged confessions.

To atone for this deplorable moment of weakness, he declared himself ready to sacrifice his life. He knew the fate that awaited him. Immediately after this unexpected coup-de-théâtre he was arrested as a relapsed heretic with another dignitary who chose to share his fate, and by order of Philip they were burned at the stake before the gates of the palace.

This brave death deeply impressed the people, and, as it happened that the pope and the king died shortly afterwards, the legend spread that the grand master, in the midst of the flames, had summoned them both to appear, within the year, before the tribunal of God.

Such was the tragic end of the Templars. If we consider that the Order of Hospitallers finally inherited, although not without difficulties, the property of the Templars and received many of its members, we may say that the result of the trial was practically equivalent to the long-proposed amalgamation of the two rival orders.

For the Knights (first of Rhodes, afterwards of Malta) took up and carried on elsewhere the work of the Knights of the Temple.

This formidable trial — the greatest ever brought to light whether we consider the large number of accused, the difficulty of discovering the truth from a mass of suspicious and contradictory evidence, or the many jurisdictions in activity simultaneously in all parts of Christendom from Great Britain to Cyprus — is not yet ended.

It is still passionately discussed by historians who have divided into two camps, for and against the order. To mention only the principal ones . . .

. . . the following find the order guilty: Dupuy (1654), Hammer (1820), Wilcke (1826), Michelet (1841), Loiseleur (1872), Prutz (1888), and Rastoul (1905); and

. . . the following find it innocent: Father Lejeune (1789), Raynouard (1813), Havemann (1846), Ladvocat

(1880), Schottmuller (1887), Gmelin (1893), Lea (1888), Fincke (1908).

Without taking any side in this discussion, which is not yet exhausted, the latest documents brought to light, particularly those recently extracted from the archives of the Kingdom of Aragon, tell strongly in favour of the order.

Grand Master Jacques de Molay

The Knights Templar
Part 2

The Knights Templar were medieval warrior monks who are regarded as legends of the Middle Ages.

They were holy men, but devellish fighters, sworn to poverty, but richer than kings.

They were believed to have guarded the most holy of relics in all of Cristendom, the Holy Grail. It was a treasure so priceless, it was thought to give them unrivalled strength, but at their pinnacle of power, the Knights Templar were slaughtered and their fortune disappeared.

Were they completely destroyed or did the secretive sect survive?

On March 18th, 1314 AD, Jacques de Molay, one of Europe's most powerful men, is about to be executed. The charges against him are of devil worship, sodomy and finacial blackmail.

He was one of 69 men who were burnt alive on the orders of King Philip IV of France and these men are among probably the most secretive brotherhoods in history...The Knights Templar.

During the Middle Ages, these warriors were feared, wealthy and all powerful, but in 1307 that reign came to an abrupt end when they were accused of heresy.

Under severe torture they were eventually forced to yield and confess, almost overnight 200 years of wealth and power went up in smoke.

The Knights Templar vanished from history. It was said that the source of their vast wealth was buried beneath the ruins of the old Jewish temple in Jerusalem.

It was thought to be an old ancient relic and its whereabouts remains a mystery to this day.

The Crusades

To discover the truth about the Templar's secret, one has to retrace their steps, back to their beginning around the clash of civilizations known as The Crusades.

In 1096 AD, an army of European knights marched thousands of miles to the region known then as the Holy Land. Muslim states dominated the Middle East from Persia to Spain. Pope Urban II called for a holy war to liberate Christianity's most sacred city, Jerusalem.

It took the crusaders about 3 years to reach the holy city, for along the way, battle, disease and starvation took their toll. A total of 4,000 knights had initially set out for Jerusalem, but only a little over 1,000 actually made it all the way to the city, Jerusalem.

In July 1099, the crusaders attacked the city and after a 5 week long seige, they succeeded in taking Jerusalem from the Muslims. It had been a bloodbath of enormous proportions, the crusaders slaughtered everyone from Muslim to Jew and Christian alike.

A French eyewitness named Raymond of Aguilers, chronicled what he saw:

"Piles of severed heads, hands and feet were to be seen in the streets of the city. In the temple and porch of Solomon, men rode in blood up to their knees and bridle reigns. It was indeed a just and splendid judgement of God, that this place should be filled with the blood of unbelievers, since it had suffered so long from their blasphemies".

To reign over the new realm of Jerusalem, the crusaders chose from within their own rank, as crusader kings fought many battles to hold this sacred ground.

In 1118, they chose their third leader, King Baldwin II. He was offered help from a crusader knight, the French nobleman Hugh de Payens.

Birth of the Templars

It was Hugh de Payens who proposed that a division of fighting warrior monks should guard the Holy Land and safeguard the passage of pilgrims on their way from Europe to Jerusalem, which they would passionately defend.

King Baldwin liked the idea and the Templar Knights were born. Initially from a band of only 9 knights, the Templar army swelled to thousands.

They officially called themselves the Order Of The Poor Knights Of The Temple Of Solomon, but over time they would simply be known as, The Knights Templar.

These knights were not only warriors, but also monks who took vows of poverty, celibacy, and obedience.

Europe had never before seen such a force, their existence was unique and revolutionary in the church.

They regarded their very being as a holy calling and they prayed over their weapons to their God.

They were considered an extremely efficient, highly disciplined and well-equipped fighting force.

They crushed the Muslims at the seige of Askaron in 1153, the Battle of Montgisard in 1177 and again at the Battle of Arsuf in 1191, the Templars now seemed invincible.

They fought by the strictest of rules, never retreating unless they were ordered to do so, and only when outnumbered by more than 3-1.

The red cross of the Templars was a sign of martyrdom. Death in battle was seen as all glorious, and their many victories in battle had earned them a sense of aura and mystique.

The Ancient Temple

This mystique grew in part from their headquarters, the Ancient Jewish Temple, given to them by King Baldwin II. Jesus himself once preached there, but it was what the Templars uncovered there that may well have shaped their destiny.

Beneath the ancient temple, legend has it that the

knights made one of the most remarkable discoveries in history.

The temple, built by King Solomon in the 10th century BC, was destroyed 400 years later by the Babylonians, and then the Jews rebuilt it.

It was once believed to house the sacred Ark of the Covenant, or Lost Ark as it is sometimes referred to today. In 70 AD, the temple was once again destroyed by war, when a Roman Army crushed a Jewish rebellion. The Romans burned the city down and destroyed the temple.

By the time of the first crusades, the Muslims had built a mosque on the site of the ruins of the Jewish temple, which still stands today.

Some historian, and scholars as well, dispute that the Knights Templar's original mission was to safeguard pilgrims to the holy Land, raising the question, what else where they doing there?

The knights spent the following 9 years tunneling through solid rock beneath the temple, and what they allegedly discovered has been a matter of intense speculation ever since.

The Dead Sea Scrolls

According to one theory, The Knights Templar discovered a treasure map detailing the exact location of the treasures of the Jewish Temple.

Back in 70 AD when the Roman Army conquered Jerusalem, Jewish rebels hid the treasures of the temple in various locations throughout the Holy Land, and in order to recover them they had made this map, etched in copper, to last forever.

The scrolls' existence was unknown for centuries, until in 1947, a Bedouin shephard looking for a stray lamb, discovered the nearly 2,000 year old maps, the Dead Sea Scrolls, and the oldest Jewish texts ever found.

One of these texts was known as the Copper Scroll and it listed a series of sites throughout the Holy Land where the temple treasures were said to have been buried.

In the 1950's a British archaeologist followed the clues etched on the Copper Scroll. He didn't find any Jewish treasure, but learned that a previous expedition discovered something just as fascinating.

He had uncovered clues that suggested someone might well have beaten him to it, fragments of swords, medieval spurs, and a red Templar cross were all discovered.

Royal Blood

Legends state that in the very ruins of the temple, the Copper Scroll led the Templars to one of Christendom's most sought after treasures...The Holy Grail.

The Grail is the subject of countless quests throughout the Middle Ages and in most legends it is either a cup or plate used by Christ at the Last Supper.

But with very little clues, its actual matter could be anything.

Other legends state that it was a stone that fell from

Heaven, and another legend connects the Grail to the very death of Jesus, the actual Roman spear that pierced Christ's side.

The most controversial theory however, is that the treasure that the Templars found may have been knowledge, knowledge suggesting towards the existence of the blood descendants of Christ.

In this theory, the Latin words for Holy Grail - SAN GREAL - is a mispronunciation of the two words SANG REAL meaning Royal Blood.

According to this theory, Jesus married Mary Magdalene and had children, these offspring are said to be the secret of the Grail. This theory of a "Royal Bloodline" may seem more plausible than a relic being the source of Templar power.

If this theory is true, it would shake the very foundations of Christianity and threaten the entire power structure of medieval Europe.

What's more, the Church would surely pay any price to keep this information an undiscovered secret.

The Templar Rise To Power

Nobody knows what the Templars may have found, but there is little argument over what happened next.

Hugh de Payens, the head of the Knights Templar, left the Holy Land to attend the council of Troyes in France.

Although it isn't stated what was debated at the meeting, the outcome is clear. Pope Honorious II gave the Templars a blessing and his successor, Pope Innocent, gave them unparalleled power.

The Knights Templar now posess immunity from laws, taxes and regulations of every nation and they subsequently become a force unto themselves.

Their mysteriously new found power, gave rise to many conspiracy theories. Modern day books like The Da Vinci Code believe that the Templars blackmailed the Vatican, demanding special priviledges for surpressing the information concerning Christ's bloodline.

However, most scholars and historians suggest that the templar's power was merely them having "good connections". Evidence of their financial power still stands today.

Most of the 12th and 13th century Gothic cathedrals, still standing today, are believed to have been financed and constructed by the Templars.

One of the finest examples of thse is the London Temple in Britain's capital. It openly displays the Templar Seal, a statue of two men riding on a single horse.

Unlike most medieval churches, this church is round.

The London Temple was designed to recreate the sanctity of the Holy Sepulcher in Jerusalem, the destination of every pilgrim and the most sacred location on earth.

The First Credit System

The London Temple wasn't just a church, it was a treasury. One king of England in 1307, went there and took £50,000 sterling. It was like walking into Fort Knox and walking off with the gold. Huge resources were being managed and administered, apparently honestly and effectively by the Templars.

The cash-rich knights began to lend money to cash-strapped nobles, they had an edge over other lenders as they could charge interest. Very few people in Europe in the Middle Ages were allowed to transact business with interest as this was seen as a sin.

Simony and usury, gaining money with interest, was severly frowned upon. The Templars may have even invented the check and credit systems.

Pilgrims travelling to the Holy Land or elsewhere would deposit money into a local Templar treasury, in return they would be given a receipt for the amount of money that had been deposited there.

Once the pilgrim had reached his destination, he would then go to the local treasury and cash in what was effectively a medieval traveller's check, or an early letter of credit. This system was convenient, but expensive, for the Templars charged up to 10% for this service.

They had originally vowed themselves to a life of

poverty, but that didn't effect their "bottom line".

Although the knights upheld their vow of poverty, individually, and they themselves did not own property, the order as a whole were allowed to store their vast wealth, and conduct their own businesses.

By the late 1200's, the Knights Templar had become the richest and most powerful organisation in Europe. However, envy and anger followed them and a ruthless plot was set in motion.

The Templar's Downfall

The crusades had made the Knights Templar their reputation, and the crusades are also about to destroy them as Muslim armies converge on the Holy Land.

After 200 years of warfare, Muslims are united under the Egyptian Sultans, and support for the crusades is dwindling in Europe.

Over time the crusades had come to be seen as too high an expense of both resources and lives. Muslims crushed the crusaders at the battles of Jaffa, El Mansoura and the seige of Safed.

By 1290, the Templars only hold one castle in the Holy Land, and at the siege of Acre in 1291 they lose that one too, and the Holy Land becomes once again occupied by Muslims.

The Templars retreated to Cyprus and after the fall of Acre, there was an overall sense of disillusionment with the idea of the crusades, due to its consumption of overstretched resources being wasted on what was increasingly being seen as futile wars.

The role of the Templars themselves is now less tenable.

History of World Banking

The Knights Templar
Part 3

After the fall of Acre in 1291, the position of the Knights Templar has become untenable and the support for any more crusades has diminished. The future of the order now lies with its new leader Jaques de Molay, but the vengeful French King Philip IV has his own plans for the increasingly unpopular knights.

The Templar's Destruction

The fate of the Knights Templar is now in the hands of it's new leader Jaques de Molay, he lobbies for support of a new crusade initiated from Cyprus, but to no avail.

De Molay travels to the Paris headquarters of the Knights Templar, on the invitation of Pope Clement V, to discuss the Templar's finances and to reassess their future endeavors. Coincedentally, Philip IV of France just happens to be in Paris at the same time.

Philip was known as "The Fair", because of his handsome looks, but he had amassed huge debts due to his wars with England, and his biggest creditor was none other than the Knights Templar.

He decides to clear his debts in one ruthless stroke, by arresting the Knights Templar and seizing all of their gold.

He concocts a number of trumped-up charges and accuses them of forms of heresy.

Friday the 13th, October 1307

Some people believe this to be the day from where the modern superstition of "Friday the 13th" originates.

In just one day, Jacques de Molay and hundreds of French Templars are rounded up, and the arrests shock Middle Age Europe to the core.

The investigation of the accused begins with torture, to try and gain the Templar's confession, but not to gain the truth.

In Paris alone, over 100 templars are tortured, including their elderly Grand Master, de Molay.

There were 127 charges against the Templars, ranging from denying Christ's existence, spitting on the crucifix, deficating on the host (the wafer of bread used in Holy Communion), and homosexuality.

What Were The Templars Worshipping?

Hundreds of the Templars inevitably confessed under the extreme torture, but they also confessed to worshipping an unusual object.

Many scholars believe this to be the severed head of John The Baptist, while others suggest that this is the Holy Grail itself.

Several of the Templars confessed to worshipping the Baphomet which some suggest is a stone idol of the Devil, so King Philip linked them to Devil Worship.

Other scholars and historians are of the belief that Baphomet is a mispronunciation of Mohammed, and that the Templars were combining a number of religious traditions in their own practice.

Thousands of Templars had served for many years in the Holy Land, and it is thought that some may have accepted the religious beliefs of the Muslims.

In the early 1980's, a scholar named Hugh Schonfield made a startling claim that Baphomet is a coded message.

The Dead Sea scholar used the Atbash Cipher from biblical studies, an ancient Hebrew encoding technique dating back to 500 BC.

When the word Baphomet is put into this cipher, a new word emerges....Sophia, Greek for wisdom.

To honor wisdom was not heresy, unless the wisdom itself is heresy. Sophia is an ancient Greek name for a goddess worshipped by an early Christian sect, the Gnostics. Was Baphomet code for goddess worship?

Some scholars say that Sophia came to earth in the body of Mary Magdalene, under the "Royal Blood" theory, — that Mary Magdalene carried the bloodline of Jesus, and subsequently became the "Vessel of Holy Blood"....the Grail itself.

In their written charter, the Templars dedicate themselves, not to Jesus, but to Mary. If the Templars worshipped Mary Magdalene as equal to Jesus, it would be considered by the Church to be a kind of heresy.

However, the Templar's charter may well be dedicated to Mary, but it does not state which one, the Blessed Virgin Mary or Mary Magdalene.

The End Of The Templars

Under torture, the Templars may have confessed to worshipping an heretical goddess religion, worshipping an Idol or even a human head. But it is more likely that the Templars were innocent scapegoats for a cowardly king who wanted to wipe away his debts.

King Philip IV demanded that the heretics face justice, reluctantly the Pope agreed, and in 1314, the Knights Templar were officially disbanded.

On March 18th 1314, after 7 years of imprisonment and torture, Grand Master Jacques de Molay is executed as an unrepentant heretic. It is said that with his dying breath, de Molay put a curse on both the Pope and the King, in which he declared "In one year, I shall see you both in a tribunal before God!".

And within one year, they were both dead.

After 200 years, the Templars were no more, their castles were taken, and their vast wealth mysteriously disappeared. Ironically, King Philip IV had never layed eyes upon the treasure before it vanished, and nobody knows where it all went after the Templar's demise.

Was It The End?

It is alleged, although unsubstantiated, that two huge carts of treasure were taken out of the city of Paris, just before the arrests on Friday the 13th, 1307.

From then on, the Templars vanished from the annuls of history, but they had had adequate warning, everywhere except in France, and some Templars are thought to have survived, even some of the ones in France.

One theory claims this to be true, and one clue to the whereabouts of the treasure survives today.

Rosslyn Chapel near Edinburgh, Scotland, appears in the book The DaVinci Code as a key clue to the hiding place of the Holy Grail. A medieval church and a lost treasure might be linked by one man.

The Rosslyn Chapel, near Edinburgh, Scotland.

The chapel was built in 1446 by William St. Clair and he was a very mysterious and puzzling figure. Although he built the chapel almost 150 years after the Templars were officially disbanded, it bears a large amount of Templar symbolism.

Two riders on a single horse is a symbol of the Templars and appears in the chapel, as does the Templar's Seal, the Lamb of God holding a cross.

Throughout the chapel are mysterious stone gargoyles and engravings, symbols and signs all depicting Templar symbolisms.

The chapel's overall layout and architecture gives many clues to its inspiration, with 14 freestanding pillars, including 2 majestic pillars at the front of the chapel, it resembles the ancient Jewish Temple described in the bible as King Herod's Temple. Had William St. Clair built the chapel to directly resemble the Jerusalem Temple?

More evidence links the Rosslyn Chapel to the Templars, some have theorized that there may well be vaults or chambers below the chapel, just like at the temple in Jerusalem, and they may hold one of the world's and history's greatest mysteries in the Templar treasure, the Holy Grail, or even perhaps....nothing at all.

The secret has been speculated over for generations, everything from the mummified head of Christ, the Ark of the Covenant, to scrolls from the temple of Jerusalem. But no specific physical evidence has ever emerged to prove any of these theories.

An exploratory excavation of the chapel has been ruled out for fear of the chapel collapsing. The chapel may only be an eccentric church, or it may be a replica of the temple at Jerusalem. Whatever its purpose, Rosslyn remains as big a mystery as the Templars themselves.

Legends state that while in prison, Jacques de Molay hid all the secrets of the Knights Templars in the first three degrees of Freemasonry.

Every single Pope since Clement V has outlawed anyone calling themselves The Knights Templar, and since the legend of de Molay reached Rome, has outlawed Freemasonry.

Were theTemplars guilty of the acts they were charged of? Was Devil worship practiced as stated?

Freemasonry survives today, not because of innocence or guilt of those knights, but because like the apostle, Paul, said: "Neither powers nor principalities, shall separate me from the love of God.

Freemasonry shall live on until men shall look upon each other for their character and uprightness, rather than through prejudiced eyes and discriminating hearts.

Until then, we must fight prejudice, despotism, and all manner of evil that exists in the hearts of men. Our sword of justice and our cause is right and "IN HOC SIGNO VINCES." - "In this sign thou shalt conquer".

　　　　　History of World Banking

Execution of Jacques de Molay
Grand Master of the Templars, at Paris

On March 18, 1314, the four Knights were brought before the gates of Notre-Dame to hear their sentence: life in prison or "the wall".

De Molay and Charnay had held on until then by the promise of eventual release. They had already spent seven years in prison and had no intention of going back in despair.

In his history of the Knights, *Hospitalers of St. John of Jerusalem,* abbé Vertot, confirms that when his judges and all of Paris expected de Molay to publicly reaffirm his supposed confessions, "The people were shocked when the prisoner shook his chains, strode to the edge of the scaffold with an assured countenance, and then, raising his voice so he could be heard, shouted: *'It is just, that on such a terrible day, in the final moments of my life, I should discover the full iniquity of the lie, and that I should make the truth triumph.*

"I thereby declare, before heaven and earth and to my eternal shame, that I have committed the greatest of all crimes, by acknowledging those so darkly attributed to an Order which the truth obliges me today to recognize as innocent. I even made the confession required only to escape the pain of torture

and to sway my torturers. I know the agonies suffered by all those who had the courage to recant such confessions. But the horrid spectacle before me cannot make me reaffirm an earlier lie with a new one, on this despicable condition. I renounce with all my heart my life which has become only hateful to me. And what good would it do me to prolong days of misery that I owe only to slander?"

Famous by a birth that related him to the king, Geoffroy de Charnay, Master of Normandy and brother to the dauphin of Auvergne, confirmed this declaration and chose to repent alongside his master. The other two Knights present persisted in their confessions.

As the crowd murmured, the cardinals, themselves moved, and unwilling to decide the fate of the relapsed, handed the two last-minute confessors of truth back to the Provost of Paris.

The king was alerted, the council assembled, and the two were immediately sentenced to death – without altering the sentence of the Pope's commissioners, without a verdict from any ecclesiastical tribunal.

That same evening, a scaffold was erected on the Ile de la Cité across from the quai des Augustins. The two Templar Knights, de Molay and Charnay, were lifted up, and slowly burned at the stake.

No Italian chronicler was fooled by the shameful trial of the Templars: not Villani, nor Dino Compagni, nor Boccaccio (whose father was in Paris at the time of the trial), nor the author of the Storie Pistolesi, nor Dante (who was present at de Molay's execution).

All could see the irony of a situation where the most faithful servants of the court of Rome, the most steadfast defenders of the faith, were killed as heretics.

French writers at the time were naturally more careful and didn't dare contradict the Pope and the king. However, as one poet clearly put it, had the Templars been truly guilty of such crimes, they would have earned the torture and other "niceties" they endured.

But since God accepted them with open arms, they were perhaps not as guilty as once thought. On earth, he continued, the Pope and the king must be obeyed. But God cannot be fooled; He alone, knows the truth.

Breaking News & Events

History of World Banking

Is the Rothschild banking monopoly about to be dismantled?

Message from Benjamin Fulford, November 1, 2011.

The situation in Europe is making it clear to all but the most brainwashed that something historical is taking place. The the criminal element at the very top of the Western power structure, especially the financial system, has been cut off from their money printing machine.

As a result, the IMF and the major European and US money center banks are insolvent. No amount of lying or paper shuffling or propaganda is going to hide this fundamental truth.

The governments of Greece, Ireland, Portugal, Italy, etc., know that the debts they supposedly owe to bankers were created through fraudulent book entries and thusly do not have to be repaid.

This is why the banks suddenly announced that Greece only had to pay back 50% of their debt, even though such a write off would destroy the banks. They are hoping for a tax payer bail-out that is just not going to happen. It is game over. The Rothschild banking nightmare is ending.

Even the highly brainwashed priesthood known as Western financial journalists and gurus are starting to realize that something is not right. The big announcement by European governments of a "solution" to the Greek and Euro crises is a case in point.

If you analyze the announcement you realize that essentially the banks and the governments are saying that the banks will pay for 50% of the Greek debt with money they do not have. The governments say they will pay for it by "leveraging" the money they already have. They do not say who is going to be dumb enough to finance a bankrupt gambler who wants to quadruple his risk.

Please note that as soon as the "solution" to the crisis was announced, high level begging missions were sent to Asia, including French President Sarkozy. Why would they need to go to Asia to ask for money if they had come up with a solution?

The IMF, supposedly the world's "lender of last resort" is also continuing to admit that they have no money. The reason is that the IMF itself cannot prove that its money comes from legitimate sources.

The fact of the matter is that the criminal part of the world's financial system is falling apart. The IMF will soon cease to be solvent. The same is true of the World Bank. The BIS is also in trouble. In fact, the entire Rothschild banking monopoly is in deep trouble.

The freeze of "trading platforms" remains in place, meaning that the controllers of the fiat system can no longer pump new money into the system. The best they can do is reshuffle money that is already in the system.

New money will only start entering the global financial system once the new asset-backed system is in place.

"The IMF and the World Bank existed to force the Rothschild banking system onto the countries of the world," is how an extremely senior Chinese official explained the situation.

"Our goal is to reboot the system, to start over and set all the parameters in a fair way so that all countries benefit from the pooled assets of the people of the world and not just Europe and North America," he continued.

"The original system was meant to have been run by the Swiss and protected by the Americans", he continued. *"The basic failure was that the system of checks and balances failed and the people who were supposed to protect the system ended up abusing it,"* he added.

What is now going to happen is that the 100 countries that have so far joined the new system started in Monaco in August, are going to implement the new system in four stages, according to a White Dragon Society source.

"The US military and agencies will be involved in this process right from the beginning", he added.

Efforts to intimidate generals by using corrupt institutions like the IRS to try to repossess their homes will backfire and lead to criminal prosecutions.

The first step will be a lawsuit that will be filed before November 15th against the individuals and groups who abused the Federal Reserve Board system. This will lead to liens being placed against many of the largest financial institutions in the world, according to the filers. There will also be mass arrests.

The other steps have yet to be disclosed. However, some basic truths are already known.

First of all, all honest businessmen and bankers worldwide will have nothing to worry about.

Second of all, the money created through derivatives fraud will be eliminated from the books, even if that means bankrupting many of the big Western financial institutions.

Third, major historical financial injustices will be addressed, and stolen monies and assets will be returned to their rightful owners. This will be good news for the vast majority of Western citizens as well as the inhabitants of long exploited regions like Africa.

The international banking and payment settlements systems will remain in place after the reboot. This will mean the minimum possible disruption to legitimate business.

However, as mentioned earlier, the international institutions, set up and controlled by a small group of Western oligarchs after WWII, will be totally revamped.

"The march of mind and of honest investigation will bring the hour when the people will chain, with fetters of some sort, the growing occultism of this period."

— *M.B.E.*

History of World Banking

The Cabalists struggle in vain to stop the new financial system

Message from Benjamin Fulford, November 15, 2011.

Despite seeming bad news on several fronts last week, insiders assure us that plans for a new financial system are going ahead on all fronts. Instead of perpetual war and genocide on behalf of an inbred elite, the people of the planet are choosing to end poverty, stop environmental destruction and push for a new life-centered scientific and technical revolution.

Major assistance emerged as a 59-nation group claiming to represent the Red Dragon Society or Maiona, offered its support to the new system.

The Red Dragon is headed by Admiral Heemi Hau, Paramount Chief of the NGAPUHI in New Zealand and links 59 countries plus 2700 tribes mostly in the South Pacific Region. They back their words with treaties with the British Empire going back to the 1700's as well as older treaties going back to 804 CE.

This is yet another step in the unstoppable global awakening that will forever take control of the planet out of the hands of the gangsters who have been terrifying us for so long.

Here is a part of what the Maiona group proposes —

Our objective is to overcome scarcity and provide for the needs of all the world's people through the creation of a sustainable, living, vibrant civilization that will eliminate all wars, fears, poverty and hunger.

Resources will be assessed globally to cover the needs of the total populations' requirement for housing, food, water, health, transport, education and recreation, and will also be co-ordinated with the needs of other species that make up the web of life on the planet.

Sources of energy will be explored and developed, but will not be limited to, wind, ocean tides, currents, temperature differentials, falling water, geothermal, electrostatic, hydrogen, algae, biomass, gravity, bacteria, phase transformation, thermionics, magnification and fusion energy.

Cities can be constructed circular, linear, underground, floating or underwater, but will all be built utilizing better resource and construction techniques. These cities would all have the ability to supply their own nutritional requirements, giving independence and sustainability.

Geometrically elegant arrangements, parks, gardens, reefs all designed to operate with efficient uses of energy and resources that co-exist with their natural surroundings. Design and development must work in with the environment providing clean air, water, food, health, nutrition, entertainment, accessibility, care and education.

This is the sort of thinking that the gangsters who took over the global financial system have proven themselves to be incapable of. They talk instead of never ending "wars on terror," and "homeland security," and "threat levels," while pouring all of the planet's free resources either into a massive military-industrial murder machine or a decadent lifestyle for a tiny elite.

These gangsters, for their part, made a big push last week in an effort to make it seem like they were still in charge. In Europe they placed cabal flunkies in power in Greece and Italy after threatening the previous democratically elected leaders into resigning. This show of force, however, is still not backed by any show of money.

The Rothschild/Rockefeller cabalists remain bankrupt and any attempts at asserting control in Europe will fail. In fact, the Greeks have contacted the White Dragon Society to inform them they will pretend to go along with the cabalists in order to get a new hit of paper money but that when the time comes to pay back, they will, as the Irish did, demand proof that the bankers had a legal right to lend that "money" in the first place.

In Japan as well, there were signs that all was not well. J. Rockefeller, one of the masterminds of the Tsunami, earthquake and nuclear attacks against Japan was spotted making a tour of the disaster zone and promising "assistance."

At the same time, the monster-toad Henry Kissinger was paraded on Japanese TV on November 11th, talking to Japanese Prime Minister Yoshihiko Noda. However, Noda lived up to his name, which means "does not give," in Spanish and Kissinger and Rockefeller left Japan empty handed.

IMF Director Christine Lagarde also returned empty-handed from her week long begging tour of Russia, China, and Japan. No doubt had it been explained to her that the 1.1 billion people who did not have enough food to eat were a greater priority than underfunded pensions for prematurely retired Europeans.

While here, Kissinger tried to hire gangsters to kill this writer but found no takers according to Japanese underground sources. Now that Kissinger's fraudulent mirror account trading platforms have been shut down it seems that his funny money is no longer accepted by the underworld here.

In other news, an informant approached this writer last week with new details about the 1995 incident in which the Aum Shinrikyo sect released poison gas in the Tokyo subway system.

The informant claims she was kidnapped, drugged, raped and tortured into becoming a MK-ultra type agent for North Korean gangsters. She said the North Koreans were taking orders from Jewish Al-Qaeda type agents.

The entire subway incident was engineered to "terrorize the Japanese," she claims. The informant provided this writer with specific names and contact information of the gangsters involved. According to her, and other sources, these same gangsters had foreknowledge of the March 11, 2011 tsunami, earthquake, and nuclear attacks on Japan.

The White Dragon Society is contacting these gangsters to try to see if they will be willing to testify about 3/11 and the Aum incident in exchange for immunity.

Needless to say the Japanese security police have also been informed.

However, according to sources among both the yakuza and Japanese military intelligence, senior members of the Japanese police forces have also been working for the cabal and have been bribed and blackmailed in the past so it is unlikely we will see any official police action on 3/11 just yet.

Nonetheless, the Japanese police/military/gangster nexus is now refusing to accept new assignments from the cabalists. Most are sitting on the fence and waiting to see how the battle for control of the global financial system turns out.

On that front, the only thing that is certain is that the old system is mathematically doomed. The criminal cabal in Wall Street, the Vatican, Washington D.C. and the "City of London" financial district know their time is up but they remain arrogant, stubborn, and dangerous.

Nonetheless, more than 107 countries have agreed to the new financial system discussed in Monaco in August. In addition, the 59-nation Red Dragon group is also working with the White Dragon. That means at least 166 nations now support the new system.

The global human awakening will not be stopped!

Rothschild family representative leaves Japan, empty handed, and makes threats

Message from Benjamin Fulford, November 21, 2011.

A senior representative of the Rothschild banking family was in Japan earlier this month demanding money, according to a high level source in the Ruling Democratic Party of Japan.

When he was told the Rothschild's Japanese piggy bank was now cut off to them, he threatened to have Japan sued for releasing radio-activity into the ocean.

The fact the Rothschilds have had to sink to such low level threats is a clear sign that they are suffering from a serious power loss. The Rothschilds need to realize that if they are to sue anybody for the Fukushima nuclear disaster, it would be their erstwhile US allies like Henry Kissinger, J. Rockefeller, and the usual Council on Foreign Relations suspects.

In any case, this ruling party source has now confirmed what multiple other sources say and that is that Senator J. Rockefeller, Henry Kissinger and now Jacob Rothschild have all visited Japan during the past month and have all left empty-handed.

There was a show-down in the Japanese underworld and the criminals who had been sub-contracting here for the Rockefellers and Rothschilds, etc., agreed to stop working for them. That is why Emperor Akihito suddenly went to the hospital and ceded responsibility to crown Prince Naruhito. This was to make sure that there was no royal family member available for these Bilderberg thugs to threaten and bully.

As a result of this underground change, the White Dragon Society has now been given detailed information about politicians who have been bribed in the past by the Sabbatean Jewish gangsters.

Some of the main conduits for Rockefeller/Rothschild bribe money included former Prime Minister Yasuhiro Nakasone, DPJ power broker Ichiro Ozawa and Tokyo governor Shintaro Ishihara. These people are now being isolated from the Japanese power structure.

In addition, the specific North Korean, Japanese and CIA operatives responsible for the 3/11 Earthquake, Tsunami, and Nuclear attacks on Japan have been identified. A representative of this group contacted the White Dragon Society to say that while they were not proud of what they had done, they had no choice but to follow orders or be killed.

Their identities have been given to sources in MI6, the CIA, Interpol, the Yakuza, the Triads and the Japanese military police. However, so long as they refrain from any *further* such operations, they will not be prosecuted but will be asked in the future to testify in front of a truth and reconciliation committee.

Also, some very esoteric financiers have emerged from the background as a result of this power shift. We will not name them for now other than to mention they are ancient European royal family foundations that have managed to keep their names out of the headlines even as the Bilderbergers and Rothschilds have had theirs dragged out and excoriated in public.

Connected to this there is once again talk of trillions of dollars being readied for the good of the planet. Talk is cheap, however, and until the money is actually spent on ending poverty, stopping environmental destruction and doing other good things for the planet, it remains just that, talk.

It is still not clear when, exactly, the new financial system will be up and running. A land-mark lawsuit that was supposed to break the ice was promised for last week but it has failed to materialize.

The bad guys, for their part, are circling the wagons in Europe, Wall Street, and Washington D.C. Vast fraud continues to be reported at the various big US and European money-center banks as well as at many of the financial exchanges. Cabal controlled governments have also been popping into existence in Spain, Italy, Greece and no doubt elsewere soon too.

However, the hard reality is that Germany alone does not have enough money to save the EU and the Euro project. The only European power with enough cash to save the day is Russia. That is why analysts in Asia expect Russia and Germany will eventually forge a Eurasian Union.

Without Russian or Asian money, the North American and European powers are now in a Wiley Coyote situation.

For those of you who never saw Road Runner cartoons as a child, Wiley Coyote would often run off a cliff and keep running in mid-air, for a while, before looking down, realizing he had no ground under his feet and falling.

Creating money out of thin air by putting numbers on computers is not reality. Unless they embrace world peace, the Washington and EU political apparatuses will crash-land.

The Pentagon, at least, has shown that it knows what the future holds. The fact of the matter is that the center of gravity of the world has shifted to Asia, and the United States military industrial complex needs to attach itself to Asia in order to survive.

The decision announced last week to permanently station US troops in Australia is part of a shift from defending Europe from Russia to defending the Chinese periphery from China. Countries like Vietnam, Korea, Japan and Thailand appreciate the economic good times the China boom has brought them, but they are also willing to hire US troops to ensure their independence.

The Chinese, for their part, understand that time is on their side, and the wiser leaders there accept the need for a gradual transition of the US military industrial complex into a peaceful organization devoted to planetary defense and exploration of the universe.

All that said, the current US regime is in no position whatsoever to lecture China about human rights when Obama himself has declared the right to kill American citizens without any trial or legal process.

The so-called Patriot act in the US is identical to the Nazi fascist constitution and the fact of the matter is that US is now ruled by a fascist regime.

Democracy is not possible in the US with rigged electronic polling and when over 90% of the media there is owned by five companies all controlled by the fascist oligarchs. Also, Australian Anzus agents have given me evidence that your Prime Minister, Julia Gillard, was undemocratically placed in power by agents of the privately owned US Federal Reserve Board.

To conclude, a peaceful transition of the military industrial complex is needed to prevent world war, and getting Asian finance for the pentagon is essential to that transition.

My understanding is that as a part of that transition, the Pentagon and the US agencies will be restoring constitutional democracy to the United States. Australia also needs to remove the banker-selected Gillard if it wishes to safeguard its democratic traditions.

History of World Banking

The Lawsuit that could end the bankster rule of Western civilizaton

Message from Benjamin Fulford, November 24, 2011.

A lawsuit was filed today (November 23rd US time) that could end the secret government that has ruled Western civilization for at least the past 300 years.

The lawsuit claims that close to $1 trillion was stolen by, among others, UN Secretary General Ban Ki Moon and the UN, former Italian Prime Minister Silvio Berlusconi and the Italian government, Giancarlo Bruno and the Davos World Economic forum and others believed to include many of the owners of the US Federal Reserve Board.

The lawsuit was filed in New York by Neil Keenan, acting as representative of the Dragon family, a reclusive group of wealthy Asian families. This filing is the result of extensive evidence gathering by international police and law-enforcement agencies including Interpol, the CIA, the Japanese Security Police, Eastern European secret services and has the backing of the Pentagon as well as the armed forces of Russia and China.

The ultimate defendants in this legal action are believed to be the same cabal behind the assassination of US President John F. Kennedy and many other major international crimes.

This particular lawsuit was triggered by the illegal detainment of two Japanese citizens, Akihiko Yamaguchi and Mitsuyoshi Watanabe, as well as the seizure of $134.5 billion in bonds they were holding in Italy on June 3, 2009.

After the bonds were stolen, self-described 33rd degree Freemason Leo Zagami contacted this writer and said the Montecarlo P2 masonic lodge could cash the bonds with the help of Vatican banker Daniel Dal Bosco.

This writer forwarded the information, via a member of the UK Royal family, to the dragon family who entrusted a further $1 trillion worth of similar bonds to the plaintiff Neil Keenan. Keenan then, after much negotiation, entrusted the bonds to Dal Bosco.

Dal Bosco subsequently absconded with the bonds and was followed 24-hours a day by various intelligence service agents to see what he would do with them. The Dal Bosco trail led to the Davos World forum, the UN, the Italian government and the Vatican, among other places.

Following this, Keenan was approached by a who's who of powerful figures including top Vatican officials, Wall Street bankers, European nobles and former US presidents, most offering him astronomical bribes to go away. He was also poisoned with ricin and nearly killed.

According to Keenan, "The roots of this case go back to between 1927 and 1938, when, under arrangements made between T.V. Soong (Finance Minister of China) and Henry Morgethau, Secretary of the Treasury, The United States Government purchased some 50 million ounces of silver and leased vast amounts of gold from the Nationalist Chinese Government known as the

Kuomintang. For all the treasure handed in, certificates were given to those who surrendered their precious metals."

Many of the bonds seized by Dal Bosco are backed with the Chinese gold taken by the Federal Reserve Board during those years and never returned to its legal owners.

Other bonds seized were Kennedy bonds. These bonds were backed by gold held in trust for the people of the planet and were supposed to be used to finance the economic development of the world. Instead they have mostly been stolen and misused by members of the cabal that has seized control of the Western financial system on behalf of private interests.

The original signatory to the Kennedy bonds was former Indonesian, President Soekarno. Soekarno's heir Dr. Seno Edy Soekanto has given Keenan power of attorney to return their rightful owners the Kennedy bonds and other property allocated to the people of the world via something known as the global collateral accounts.

The lawsuit is only the first salvo in a legal battle to restore control of the global financial system to the people and governments of the world as well as the rightful owners of historical assets that have been seized by members of the banking cartel.

The lawsuit has been filed as **Civil Action #8500** at the United States District Court for the Southern District of New York, on November 23, 2011.

Background information on the problems with the financial system of the globe

The entire cause of the problem:

The United States is a private corporation owned by the British Crown (Rothschilds), the Bank of England (Rothschilds), and the Vatican (Rothschilds again). It was previously called the Virginia Company until 3/9/1933 when it was dissolved by Roosevelt under the Emergency Banking Act.

On 5/5/1933 Congress elected to dissolve the Gold Standard and Sovereign Authority of the U.S. and all of its official capacities including government offices, departments, and officers.

The U.S. is a corporation, not a nation. And the Federal Reserve is neither Federal, nor a Reserve. It is a private counterfeiting organization run by Jewish bankers who lend the money they print out of thin air, at interest, while we keep on paying these criminals to fleece we the People.

That technology of theft and deception that has been exported from the United States through their promotion of this fraud as the paradigm of global finance is an obscenity that has set the seeds of its own destruction.

This has been compounded by the refusal of ordinary people to realize, know and understand that it is the duplicity of Governments, and the deceit and endless greed of bankers, that combined to simply fleece them like the apathetic sheep they are.

Apathy and ignorance of the truth, creates belief in the lie. The truth is self-evident, but most people choose to neither hear it nor understand it. The debts of the Federal Reserve are the debts of a private corporation that is robbing the people of the United States.

The United States Dollar is a Federal Reserve Note and the obligations against the currency are obligations of the Federal Reserve, not of the people of the United States.

Understanding the History

Excerpts from the Complaint —

1. Between 1927 and 1938, under arrangements made between T.V.Soong (Finance Minister of China) and Henry Morgethau, Secretary of the US Treasury, The United States Government purchased some 50 million ounces of silver and leased vast amounts of gold from the Nationalist Chinese Government, known as the Kuomintang. During this period, China was partly occupied by Japanese troops and there was the fear of China being overrun by the Japanese.

2. For all the treasure handed in, certificates were given to those who surrendered their precious metals. The surrendered precious metals and gemstones were sent to the United States under a lease agreement made between T.V. Soong and Henry Morgenthau. The Certificates became the underlying funds of the Kuomintang and were good and accepted securities.

3. In 1933 a new Securities Act was promulgated in the United States, together with the Gold Act, which required all gold bullion and gold coin to be surrendered to the Federal Reserve, a private corporation chartered to operate as the Central Bank of the United States, and to be the issuer of the currency known as the United States Dollar. The gold was purchased with paper FRN's.

4. Foreign Gold held by the Treasury was also surrendered to the Federal Reserve, and was leased to it. This began the series 1934 Notes issued by the Federal Reserve. These have never been redeemed and the interest cost was met by further issuances of the 1934 series FRN's.

5. These 1934 FRN's guarantee the lease payments to the Federal Reserve and allow the Chinese Government to continue financially. These came under the control of the Kuomintang, the Nationalist Government in China from whom the Gold had been received. Many were left in China when the Kuomintang had to flee to Taiwan. The Gold had been nationalized by the Kuomintang who moved much of the FRN's (but not all) to Taiwan which was built on these notes. These Notes were the underlying wealth of Taiwan and they were good for value as they were backed by gold.

6. During the war in China, most owners of the depository notes issued by Chinese Banks were killed by the Japanese, others later being killed by both the Kuomintang and the Chinese Communists, thus the Gold became the property of the Nation, especially the Kuomintang. In Europe, Jews who had owned wealth were stripped of that wealth through various means and were then killed. The gold was taken either by stealth or by force, that is a reality of history.

7. The Kuomintang appointed guardians of this Gold and the securities issued by the United States; these guardians are euphemistically known as the Dragon Family.

The Dragon Family is in fact an organization that operates between old families within China and Taiwan, and as such is above the political divide of the two independent Chinese Governments.

The Chinese are remarkable in this regard, that old family ties and functions supercede political arrangements which, though they might last for generations, are regarded as inconsequential over the passage of time to most Chinese. Attached to this is the wealth of several nations.

The United States in support of the Kuomintang and resistance groups actually printed more of these FRN's inside China itself. These operations were run by the CIA to buy loyalty of various factions in the fight against the communists, eventually being driven out into Burma around 1960. Largely due to the additional printing of these notes, the additional Notes were given in lieu of interest, but directed to specific persons and parties.

8. At the end of the World War II, with Communist and Kuomintang factions at war in China, the International Community and the Chinese assented to the Gold being placed under the overt control of Indonesian President Soekarno. Soekarno then, on August 17, 1945, came to be known as M1 under United Nations Approval No. MISA 81704 "Operation Heavy Freedom", because much of the world's gold had been delivered into Indonesia and the Philippines. Canada, Australia, Great Britain, India, and other British Colonies sent their gold to the so called "impregnable Singapore". The Japanese, as per the arrangements agreed to by Hirohito in the 1921 Pact Between Nations made in London, delivered

much of this gold to Indonesia (Then a Dutch Colony) and to Philippines (Then a US Colony) into secret bunkers that had been mostly constructed by the Japanese between 1924 and 1945.

This is why the Allied troops in Malaya had no air cover, or sufficient supplies, that would have allowed them to resist the Japanese. Singapore had to fall so most of the global wealth could be "lost" into a secret system that made the gold standard redundant and fiat currencies a reality.

This gold was documented into accounts through the Swiss Commercial Bank and Union Bank of Switzerland, placed under protection of the Swiss Attorney General, registered through the Swiss National Bank into the Bank for International Settlements International Collateral Combined accounts, and then from within the BIS, blocked to form the Institutional Parent Registration Accounts of the Federal Reserve System.

Later President Marcos of the Philippines was appointed and held the position of M1, until 1987, and then the position was transferred to Dr. Ray C. Dam, under Legal Decadency to Heir RCD1087 Far East Entire with formal Power of Attorney and Assignment of Indonesian Assets, signed by Sarinah Soetiwi (holder of the assets on behalf Indonesia as assigned by President Soekarno) in 1992. Dam's authority later promulgated January 20, 1995. Dam proved to be impossible to work with, and his authority over the Institutional parent registration Accounts was set aside, and the system reverted to the three Nations who had controlled these accounts since World War II, United States, Great Britain, and France, who have systematically and illegally subverted the established system since 1996.

9. From this we can see that there are two functional operations. One was ownership and Depository control by the owners of the Gold, and the other a control system set in place to administer and control the Collateral Combined Accounts as an independent Arbiter. Ownership rights are held by the signatory to the Depository Accounts in Commercial Banks and Control Rights have been held by M1.

10. The entire world supply of bullion and coinage gold was withdrawn and fiat currencies became the order of the day. However, underneath the notes and money issued by the Federal Reserve was the underlying wealth within a centralized system that Nations that were intended to use it equitably, but Bankers determined they would use it to raid national economies.

11. In 1963, President John F. Kennedy entered into an Agreement with President Soekarno to provide the funds that would allow the United States Treasury to print its own currency, thus subverting the "right to print the currency" held by the Federal Reserve.

This Agreement would have transferred some 59,000 tons of gold to underpin this currency. The problem with this was that the US domestic currency would have then been backed by gold, which would have been a violation of international agreements to stabilize currencies.

Eleven days after signing this agreement, President Kennedy was assassinated. President Johnson then suspended EO11110 as issued by Kennedy and transferred the bullion to the Federal Reserve.

The Green Hilton Agreement was not implemented until 1968 when Soekarno fell from office and Global Trade made it imperative that the world would have a Global Currency.

As the Gold had been transferred to the US Treasury in 1968, a series of Bonds known as Kennedy Bonds were issued in order to honor the terms of the Green Hilton Agreement made between Kennedy and Soekarno, the 1968 terms of the gold delivery to the United States being different than that made in 1934.

When after 30 years, interest had not been paid as promised, a reissue of the bonds in an increased number were issued as commemorative notes and were accepted by the Dragon Family, the owners of the Gold.

12. From copies of Bank documents received by Neil Keenan, within the Green Hilton Memorial Agreement, the funds in the amounts of gold and platinum are specified. These amounts of gold are certificated and the certificates and ledger copies with full and exact identification and recognition codes are available. These certificates are further proven by the bank reports, copies of which are now held by Neil Keenan. The truth of these instruments can be vigorously defended through documentation in our hands and further through interrogation of the Black Screens where the off ledger collateral is held, together with an interrogation of the grey and blue screens where we will find enormous fraud from the illegal use of these assets.

13. In the few documents that we present with this complaint we can see that the assets have been deposited, the counter-assets created and presented to the

depositors, and that the depositors have been cheated for over 70 years through the intentional and fraudulent failure of the Obligor to honor the Agreements.

14. In recent weeks we have come into possession of the books and records of the late President Soekarno, and all the codes and ledgers of the Global Accounts. The size of these accounts can be seen by reviewing the Collective Agreement between the Garuda Memorial Hilton in Indonesia and the Green Memorial Hilton in Geneva, established, structured and made operational between 1961 and final signature in 1972. Under this Agreement the assets of the international collateral combined, were established, brought forward, and then, within a short period of time, misused to change the operating systems of banks.

15. Reviewing these books, we can now see that Banks set aside the notion of operating under the Charters they hold as banks, and instead of being Banks they became like poor casino operators and traders, selling what they did not own. The records in our possession, signed and registered by the receiving and managing commercial bank, show the underlying funds in numbers and amounts that stagger the imagination.

. . . here are two important videos that will help you make some sense of what we believe are the 'real' historical connections to what is going o today. The first video is short (8 minutes) and the second is long (5 hours) and could be viewed in parts over a longer period of time.

While these videos speak the larger truth, they do not necessarily show the entire picture as correct. There may be details that result from the bias of the creator, or the "real" facts may not be available as yet. After all, our history has been successfully hidden from us for far too long, so those who have the courage to dig further may not have have it absolutely correct. . . . ~DR

1. **City of London, the Vatican, and Washington, DC.**
   http://tinyurl.com/6ttdlwu

2. **Ring of Power, an epic documentary of it all!**
   http://tinyurl.com/3wb2ulf

Ring of Power: *This amazing 5 hour video provides the missing pieces of our human story from the mystery religions of ancient Egypt, to the Zionist role in 9/11. Find out how an Illuminati network of International bankers and European royalty have turned the world's nations and citizens into* their *debt slaves.*

Part 1: 9/11 The Untold Story
Half the world believes Muslims were responsible for 9/11. The other half believes it was Israeli Zionists. Who is right?

Part 2: Hidden Empire
The world's most powerful empire is not the USA. It is an empire that insiders call "Empire Of The City."

Part 3: Trail Of The Pharaohs
Did the Biblical Abraham really live to be 175? Did Moses really turn staffs into snakes and rivers into blood?

Part 4: God And The Queen
Genealogy charts show that British and French royalty are descendants of Mary Magdalene and Jesus. Is it true?

Part 5: All The Queen's Men
How rich and powerful is Queen Elizabeth II?

Part 6: The Godfathers
They scammed control of the Bank of England and the US Federal Reserve, then they found "God" — Gold, Oil, and Drugs.

Part 7: Cheating At Monopoly
How many people would play a game of monopoly if the banker was cheating and fixing the rules? Over 6 billion!!!

Part 8: Asses Of Evil

The New World Order MAFIA are invisible rulers who make puppets out of politicians and heroes out of villains.

Part 9: King Of Hearts

The ultimate goal of "insiders" is to disarm the world and create a one world empire under a one world ruler.

Who *is he*?

Part 10: Solutions

Protesting and writing letters to deaf politicians doesn't work. What *does* work?

"Lulled by stupefying illusions, the world is asleep in the cradle of infancy, dreaming away the hours. Material sense does not unfold the facts of existence; but spiritual sense lifts human consciousness into eternal Truth." — M.B.E.

History of World Banking

OTHER PUBLICATIONS

NESARA: National *Economic Security and Reformation Act*
http://tinyurl.com/c8u42q6

History of Banking: *An Asian Perspective*
http://tinyurl.com/boeehjl

The People's Voice: *Former Arizona Sheriff Richard Mack*
http://tinyurl.com/d62fyg3

Asset Protection: *Pure Trust Organizations*
http://tinyurl.com/btrjfqp

The Matrix As It Is: *A Different Point Of View*
http://tinyurl.com/ckrbkge

From Debt To Prosperity: *'Social Credit' Defined*
http://tinyurl.com/d2tjmw3

Give Yourself Credit: *Money Doesn't Grow On Trees*
http://tinyurl.com/d7tphuv

My Home Is My Castle: *Beware Of The Dog*
http://tinyurl.com/bmzxc2n

Commercial Redemption: *The Hidden Truth*
http://tinyurl.com/d9etg7w

Hardcore Redemption-In-Law: *Commercial Freedom And Release*
http://tinyurl.com/cl65vrz

Oil Beneath Our Feet: *America's Energy Non-Crisis*
http://tinyurl.com/btlzqxf

Untold History Of America: *Let The Truth Be Told*
http://tinyurl.com/bu9kjjc

Debtocracy: *& Odious Debt Explained*
http://tinyurl.com/cooqzuz

New Beginning Study Course: *Connect The Dots And See*
http://tinyurl.com/cxpk42p

Monitions of a Mountain Man: *Manna, Money, & Me*
http://tinyurl.com/cusgcqs

Maine Street Miracle: *Saving Yourself And America*
http://tinyurl.com/d4yktlw

Reclaim Your Sovereignty: *Take Back Your Christian Name*
http://tinyurl.com/cf5taxh

Gun Carry In The USA: Your Right To Self-defence
http://tinyurl.com/cdn3y3y

Climategate Debunked: *Big Brother, Main Stream Media*
http://tinyurl.com/d6gy2xz

Epistle to the Americans I: *What you don't
know about The Income Tax*
http://tinyurl.com/d99ujzm

Epistle to the Americans II: *What you don't
know about American History*
http://tinyurl.com/cnyghyz

Epistle to the Americans III: *What you don't
know about Money*
http://tinyurl.com/cp8nrh8

www.ingramcontent.com/pod-product-compliance
Lightning Source LLC
Chambersburg PA
CBHW051538170526
45165CB00002B/782